CHAPTER 1

Why are you writing a book?

Why have you written a book, or decided to write one?

Authors seeking publishers usually fall into one of two camps. In Camp One is the **book-driven** author – the person who has written, or is writing, a particular book because it needed to be written. It might be a true life story, his or her own or someone else's. It might be a book on a particular subject on which this person is an expert, and wishes to share his or her expertise and experience with a wider public. Maybe it's about a public scandal the author has been involved in, or perhaps it's an account of life-changing loss or suffering. Usually it's the only book this author intends to write (though it's not unusual for a book-driven author to get the bug, and move on to writing books for the hell of it).

At this point they move over to Camp Two – the **writing-driven** authors. These are the people who enjoy writing, feel they have some talent and would like to entertain readers with their work. Most of these authors have already written their books when they come to us for help. They don't just want a book in print – they seek recognition for it.

These two kinds of authors need to approach the business of publishing in very different ways, as I shall explain.

When English 1:1 hit the market some centuries ago, the designers should have avoided the terrible clumsiness of 'his and her' by inventing a gender-neutral singular personal pronoun. They didn't, so in addition to using both the male and female personal pronouns I will follow an increasingly common practice by using 'them', 'they' and 'their' in its place – ugly, but useful, and I suspect the day will come when it is considered correct English and no longer grates on the ear.

The book-driven author

There are lots of reasons why you might feel there is a book inside you which really needs to escape and fly out into the sunshine. Perhaps you've had a long and interesting life, and you'd like to get it down on paper. That's an excellent reason for writing a book. Many a successful man (around two thirds of the whole-life autobiographies my firm has published have been written by men), upon realising he has reached that stage of his life when most of it is behind him, decides to commit his story to paper.

Perhaps your life has been particularly challenging because of poverty or disability, racial or religious discrimination, even abuse. Your account of coping with your situation and, we hope, eventually triumphing, could make a powerful story – and perhaps more to the point, it will help you to feel more at peace with what you have had to endure. It may even help and inspire others who find themselves in the same situation.

Perhaps you have developed an expertise over many years in a particular subject to which you're devoted, such as a pastime, a person, a place, an aspect of business, an area of natural history or a sport. You may feel you've acquired a depth of knowledge which really ought to be shared with others. That's a great motive too, as your passion for your subject is likely to shine through and drive the book on, and others out there who share the same passion may be persuaded to buy it.

Possibly you wish to pay tribute to an ancestor who achieved great things, or an unsung hero who you feel deserves a biography. Such books can often work very well and will be greatly appreciated by others who knew the person in question.

The writing-driven author

Perhaps you feel you're a natural storyteller, and you want to graduate to publishing a novel, or a book of short stories. Or maybe you just love the whole wonderful business of writing, and feel you're good at it; after all, others have praised your work. Your book is your attempt to show the world what you can do with words, and perhaps win a little critical recognition. There couldn't be a finer motive – as long as you're realistic about your chances of commercial success. More about that later.

A writing-driven author may be a talent looking for a subject – you'd like to write a whodunnit, but how are you going to come up with a decent plot? You love horror stories, but how do you go about writing one that's original? It certainly makes sense to start with a genre you know. If you have been soaking up romantic fiction since your teens, you already have much of the knowledge and insight you'll need to write one yourself, though you may not realise it.

If you dream of being a successful author and aren't sure what sort of book to write, I suggest you take a look at the market, because some genres sell a lot better than others (see below). But don't make the mistake of trying to write a book you're not equipped for, just because it's high on the favourite fiction list.

Writing for money

'Almost anyone can be an author; the business is to collect money and fame from this state of being.' – A A Milne

What if you're bored with your day job, and thinking how much better life would be if you could earn a living as a writer? Or struggling to pay the rent, and hoping your writing could make you a bit of extra money? This may not be such a great place to start from. It's notoriously difficult to make money from any kind of writing, and particularly from books. But more importantly, if you're writing to make money and not from one of the above motives, what's going to breathe fire into your book – what will be the life force that makes your words sing from the page? Pounds, shillings and pence won't do that, any more than they will make you throw your heart and soul into your temporary job in the packaging department. You should be driven to write for its own sake.

Pay rates for writers in general are low, simply because words are cheap (all the more so in this age of the electronic keyboard), and there are too many people out there who want to write for a living and are willing to do it for a handshake and a ham sandwich. There are websites out there where you can register as a writer and wait for the assignments to come in. I tried this idea once, but decided that for six dollars an hour it really wasn't worth powering up my laptop (not that I could afford a laptop at the time).

So setting out to write a book just with the idea of making money is not a good starting point. But writing a book that is in your heart and which *could* make a little money, as opposed to one that may be satisfying to you but which no one will ever buy, is a more sensible proposition.

Earnings from writing

Let's take a brief look at how much writers make. While a few people at the top of the profession, those who can sell books by the tens and hundreds of thousands, earn incomes to die for, the great majority are struggling. A 2015 survey by Queen Mary University (London)* showed that only one in ten writers say they can now afford to make a living from their craft alone, down 40% on ten years ago. A typical author makes just £11,000 a year, or just over 40% of the national average wage (that's the median** figure – the average is £16,800, but that's weighted by the small number of writers who earn much more). The average professional writer earns £28,540, more encouraging but still not exactly second-home-in-the-south-of-France stuff.

There is huge inequality between the successful writers

and the rest – the top 50% of professional authors earn 93% of all the money and the top 10% earn 58% of it. In terms of genres, the academic writers are the paupers, with an average net income just over £3800. Audio-visual writers (those writing for electronic media) do best, with an average of almost £34,000, probably because their work is relatively quickly done, so they can do more of it, and because the writer's fee will look small alongside the overall budget for the production.

The good news for novelists is that the next highest spot is taken by fiction, at £28,809. But again, that's the average – when you look at the median figure, it is just £6268. In other words, a few novelists make a lot of money, but the bottom 50% earn around £6000 a year or less.

The report reveals that while life has not improved for authors in recent years, the authors themselves overwhelmingly believe that it has got worse. As the report puts it, 'It is clear that writers have a picture of the industry far bleaker than is actually the case'.

Indeed, according to a May 2016 Publisher's Association report***, the industry as a whole is now growing rather than declining. Total sales of physical books and journals increased for the first time in four years, to a value of £4.4 billion. At the same time digital sales fell, for the first time in the seven years since they were first recorded.

Not so long ago, writing a book, with all the labour and dedication it implied, seemed quite a special thing to do, like climbing Kilimanjaro for charity or learning to play the cello – 'gosh, John is writing a *book*!' Getting one published was an even greater (and rarer) achievement. Now that computers are household familiars and the internet can look after everything from checking your facts to designing your cover, everything has changed. Books are no longer being written just by dedicated writers but by anyone who wants to, regardless of literary skill and experience. Getting one published, on the other hand, has become even more difficult, unless, of course, you go the self-publishing route. More about that later.

It ought to be made into a film...

'Drive to the border of California, throw your book over the fence. When they throw the money back over the fence, collect the money and drive home.' – Ernest Hemingway

It's not unusual for an author to feel that his story is just what Hollywood is looking for, particularly if it's a colourful life story or true-life adventure. Unfortunately the film industry offers no straightforward way in; sending manuscripts to publishers is like feeding the pigeons in the park compared with getting a book in front of someone who might actually write out a cheque for the film rights. Good contacts are pretty much indispensable – you have a much better chance if you know someone who knows someone who knows the right producer. If you are serious about getting your book filmed, first take your publisher's advice as to whether it's the right sort of book (and make sure your contract gives you the film rights, or a fair proportion), then do your homework and prepare for a great deal of hard work and a long and laborious process.

The tools of the trade

A word, before we go too much further, about the technology you're likely to be using to write your book. The computer has made writing, compiling, correcting, reviewing, researching, copying and transmitting manuscripts almost indecently easy. At least, it has if you have a basic grasp of the business of using a PC or laptop. If you haven't and you're too much of a Luddite to feel confident of getting on top of it, please get someone to show you how to create, format and save a Word document (your publisher will prefer your book to be supplied to them in Word or compatible software), how to cut and paste, use a spellchecker, enter accents, colour text, use Track Changes, insert comments and attach files to emails; also how to save and catalogue images, if you're including any.

If your computer is more than a few years old, you really ought to invest in a new one; a decent laptop now costs only around £300, or half that second hand. Windows 7 is the earliest version I would recommend using (it's also currently the earliest that is still supported by Microsoft). Using outdated IT equipment and software (or almost, but not quite, compatible freeware) could turn handling your manuscript into a nightmare, and may try your publisher's patience beyond endurance. I have known authors to print out and post 200-page manuscripts because they couldn't work out how to get their computer to attach a file to an email, authors who tried to submit 100mb files (far too big for anyone to work with) because they had embedded all the pictures in the manuscript, and authors who accidentally deleted books and lost them for ever because they didn't back up, and didn't know how to recover documents. If you get into the routine of saving your file each time you finish working on it, and set up your PC to perform an automatic save every few minutes, you will never lose a manuscript, unless perhaps your hard disc crashes – and if you back it up regularly to a memory stick, an external drive, a cloud storage facility or some other medium, not even then.

The Business of Being an Author – A Survey of Author's Earnings and Contracts, Professor Johanna Gibson, Queen Mary University of London, Professor Phillip Johnson, Cardiff University and Dr Gaetano Dimita, Queen Mary University, April 2015

**The median figure is the one that separates the top 50% from the bottom.*

***www.publishers.org.uk*

CHAPTER 2

What not to write

What sort of book has a chance of showing a little payback, and what sort is destined for probable oblivion?

Exactly which kinds of books sell best depends on how you define them, but a perusal of Amazon's figures indicates that broadly the best-selling categories are as follows:

Romantic fiction (contemporary and historical)
Erotic fiction
Self-help (mind, body and spirit)
Science fiction and fantasy
Mystery fiction
Thrillers
Biographies
Health, fitness and dieting
Religion and spirituality

Now just because romantic fiction tops the list it doesn't mean that you, as an aspiring author, should whizz off and write some – you also have to factor in how many other people are competing to do the same thing. And as mentioned, you must take into account – very important, this – what kind of book you could do well. Writing a bodice-ripper because bodice-rippers sell is fine – as long as you have some idea how to do it. In fact, I'm pretty sure (never having tried to write one myself) that bodice-rippers are just as difficult to do properly as all the rest.

Try googling a few phrases like 'best-selling books 2016' or 'amazon best sellers' to explore what's selling and what isn't. You'll get a range of confusing, often conflicting, information, but it will give you some useful clues. There's some information about what's been selling, over the decades and more recently, in Appendix II.

The vital ingredients

What does a book need to be successful? Three key ingredients can be singled out:

Excellence. Trade publishers will not accept anything that isn't very good indeed; if it's a novel, it must be a really compelling story, well written, with strong, original characters. Remember that if you're writing a thriller, the readers you're targeting could buy a John Grisham for the same money, and if you're writing a bonkbuster, you're asking them to buy your book instead of a Jilly Cooper or a Jackie Collins. You are also asking them to devote valuable hours of their lives to your book, when they could be reading something else – or doing something else.

Differentness. Many a new author believes his book is original when it really isn't. For a book to sell it needs to be talked about, and to be talked about it needs to be remarkable in some way, usually through an exceptionally inventive (but credible) plot, a marvellous title, a compelling lead character or a gripping story idea (a horse that goes to war, a man marooned on a desert island). In the film world such 'big idea' stories are often referred to as 'high concept'. The higher your concept (as long as it's credible) the better the chance of your book being talked about and bought. The lower the concept – the more conventional the story – the more likely it is that no one will take the slightest notice.

Targeting. Just as marketing people design products to meet specific, identified needs (food you can eat on the go, non-iron shirts), publishers choose books to meet current reader demand. The better you understand what that means, the better chance your book has of being at least considered for publication. A common problem with books submitted to Mereo is that they cross genres – a light comedy which contains passages of soft porn, a memoir which follows six chapters about a sun-kissed country childhood with fifteen more dealing with a meteoric career in finance. Study the list of genres at the end of this book and ask yourself which your book, whether its fact or fiction, belongs to – and it should be one only. Otherwise it's going to be like trying to market a brand of cereal which also makes really good cushion stuffing.

Keep it (reasonably) short

'There should be a law establishing 20,000 words as the target length for a book – if you write more, you get taxed so much

per word. We'd all get through life a lot quicker' – Michael Frayn

There's a tendency for the real humdinger best-sellers to look more like doorsteps than books; Tolkien's The *Lord of the Rings* and Tolstoy's *War and Peace* both contain in the region of half a million words, and both have sold many millions of copies. Interestingly, a trend is being reported towards longer books; according to the eBook specialist Smashwords in their 2016 market survey, their top 100 bestsellers averaged 112,000 words, and their top 1,000 bestselling books averaged over 103,000 words. But don't let this entice you as a new author into thinking your book should be long. It's nice to offer your readers value for money, if your book really needs to be long, but if it's going to be self-published (like most) it'll cost you. It will take an editor four times as long to sort out a book of 200,000 words as one of 50,000, and print and P&P costs may force a higher cover price than readers are prepared to pay. At the other end of the scale, though Michael Frayn no doubt made the comment above with tongue in cheek (his own novels are a great deal longer than 20,000 words), anything much less than about 30,000 words may leave the reader feeling short-changed, particularly if it's a novel. For most books, around 50-100,000 words is a good target to aim for.

Choose your genre

At Mereo we see a constant flow of manuscripts from hopeful authors; some we publish, after suitable editing, some we don't. They vary enormously, from the unputdownable to the unreadable, but whether they are literary *tours de force* or incoherent nonsense, they can broadly be categorised as follows:

Romance

Romantic fiction, either contemporary or historical, has been a top seller for centuries and its position at the top of the list seems secure. But standards are high and competition is fierce. Not many new authors manage to come up with the characters, the storyline and the deft command of prose required to make it to the top. But much of this comes with practice; authors with talent who listen to their editors and keep working at it may eventually write a book that makes a splash.

Erotica

This is a large and booming market, particularly in eBooks, thanks partly to the growing acceptance of erotic fiction as respectable reading matter for women, the main buyers. The boom didn't begin with *Fifty Shades of Grey* in 2012, but that title certainly gave it a massive shot in the arm. It sent publishers scrambling to join the bandwagon, which according to media reports put a big dent in other genres – not so much because readers started reading steamy fiction instead of their usual books but because publishers started favouring erotica submissions at the expense of the rest. If sexy stories are your bag as a writer, you could do worse than have a go. But make sure you know the difference between a steamy but supermarket-friendly erotic novel and top-shelf hardcore pornography, which is a specialist market, not handled by most publishers – at least not under their usual imprint.

Poor writing is as unforgivable in this genre as in any other. According to Claire Siemaszkiewicz of erotica specialist Totally Bound Publishing, there's a serious lack of well-written erotic romance; their research shows that the single biggest turn-off for UK readers is poorly-written prose (source: Publishing Perspectives).

Fantasy and science fiction

J R R Tolkien has a lot to answer for, in the view of those who despise all fantasy fiction and the countless films and computer games based upon it. But lots of people are hooked on it, and will read even the most derivative sagas if they read well. If this is your genre, I suggest you go right ahead with your book, but please read Chapter 6 first. It's unlikely you will want to embark on a fantasy novel unless you're already a fan of the genre and an avid consumer. You certainly have no chance if you're not.

Science fiction and fantasy both have the advantage that if you can create an enthralling, believable world and set of characters in Book One and start collecting some readers, you can keep on feeding them more. The late Terry Pratchett's Discworld series added up to 41 books and 80 million sales, Frank Herbert's Dune books did even better, and you don't need me to tell you what happened to Harry Potter or Frodo Baggins.

Ghost stories and horror

These are genres which enjoyed their glory days in the Victorian and Edwardian eras, and works by the likes of M R James, Algernon Blackwood, Lady Cynthia Asquith, Edgar Allan Poe, H P Lovecraft and William Hope Hodgson continue to send shivers down our spines a hundred years on. Fine ghost stories are still being written of course. Great fun to write, and if your ideas are original enough, you might find some readers. Again, see Chapter 6.

True crime

This is a good subject, as it's a perennial top seller. It's best to pick an interesting and preferably under-explored crime, perhaps one that has been forgotten for a generation or two, and equally important that you do your homework. If the crime and criminal have passed into legend there will be anoraks out there who have been studying the subject for years and read everything published about it, and if you get your facts wrong or jump to conclusions on poor evidence, they will pounce, and probably trash your book on Amazon. Best to pick an interesting crime which has not been done to death, if you'll forgive the expression, and go to the most authoritative sources, then check as much as possible. But again, you need an angle – no point in telling an old story without something new to add.

The Mereo title *An Unjust Hanging* (Dave Halliwell, 2012) told how the descendants of a young man hanged for murder nearly two centuries ago established that he had been the victim of a cruel justice system and an unscrupulous surgeon – a great story, full of revelation, which attracted considerable media attention, helping to bring sales for the book. *A House to Remember* (Edna Gammon, 2011) put a new slant on the story of the notorious murders by John Christie at 10 Rillington Place in the 1950s, presenting the evidence that Timothy Evans, widely considered to have been unjustly hanged, had indeed killed his wife and child.

Whole-life memoirs

Mereo was founded as Memoirs Books, because we assumed that people's memoirs would form our core business. The reality has proved to be more interesting and much more varied, as you will see, but memoirs are still very important to us.

Most autobiographies we see are full-length life stories by people who have had varied and interesting lives, typically people who have retired after long and successful business careers. The tone and content varies according to the author's personality and intentions, but such books are characterised by a sense that the writer wishes to set down on paper a life which perhaps is not far from its end, to crystallise precious memories and pass them on to loved ones and descendants, and to relive past adventures and glories through the act of writing them down.

A personal memoir is not generally written to make money, as the author recognises that only people who know him are likely to read it; the more realistic may acknowledge that even their wives and children might not read the book from cover to cover, particular if it is a long book and full of detailed accounts of long-ago boardroom battles and financial shenanigans. Even autobiographies by famous people don't sell well unless they can offer at least one of the vital ingredients – revelation (the more scandalous the better), humour and a gripping story.

Family histories

Many a writer wishes to chronicle the family's history or paint a biographical portrait of a recent, revered ancestor, and because of where we happen to be in time, that means, more often than not, someone who served in one of the two great wars of the 20th century. Mereo has published many such books, and they are often fascinating reading. The diary of a humble private who served on the Somme in 1914 is a harrowing yet heart-warming read, particularly as this particular private happened to be unusually gifted with the pen. A book about an aviation pioneer is a more high-flown work in both senses, while an account of a British officer who suffered appalling privations as a prisoner of the Japanese in Burma, while gruelling, ultimately raises one's faith in the nobility of the human race. The story of a particular regiment and its deeds in battle will be fascinating for those whose relatives have served in the same 'firm'.

These books may be of genuine historical interest and are well worth setting down on paper. They may also sell well, to those whose interest is military history, if they are revealing and well written. However, there are a lot of them about, so please don't assume that just because your uncle was there when the Allies landed in Normandy on D-Day, his book will be a big seller. It will still have to be a good read.

Biographies of famous people

The word 'famous' is key here. If you write about someone who isn't famous at all except to a tiny group of followers, only the members of that small and diminishing band are ever likely to buy it. On the other hand, if you choose someone who is genuinely famous, there will already be biographies out there and you will probably find it hard to tell the world anything new unless you really were Monty's double or Madonna's road manager. A biography may well have a guaranteed audience of waiting readers – it's just that it could be a very small one. So pick your subject with care, if sales are important to you. And of course your approach to the book will depend on whether you are writing it for them, despite them or after they have passed away.

Of course the lives of famous people are not necessarily interesting, and many very interesting people are not at all famous. You need a bit of both for a book to be successful.

Don't make the common mistake of assuming that if you're writing about the life of Cameron McGilligan, all the members of the Cameron McGilligan Society, everyone who ever met Cameron McGilligan and most of those who have read his books/enjoyed his music/patronised his restaurant will buy your biography. Unfortunately, most people just aren't that interested in reading books.

A well-written life is almost as rare as a well-spent one – Thomas Carlyle

Survival and bereavement

Many people write books as a way of coming to terms with an ordeal they have had to go through, often in childhood; indeed quite a few authors have told us that a doctor or counsellor had advised them to write about their experiences as a form of therapy. Such stories often concern a disabling medical condition or some form of childhood abuse. At their best, they are moving and inspiring, but they can make grim reading. Such authors often say they want to write a book so that people like them will know they are not alone, or so that people will realise how widespread their problem is. That's a great motivation, but I would caution against expecting too many people to buy a book on such a difficult subject.

Books about someone who died too soon, usually written, consciously or otherwise, as part of the bereavement recovery process, are often very moving. Such a book is invariably a tribute to someone from whose loss the writer will never fully recover. They are not written with a view to making money, and very often the writer stipulates that the proceeds from sales should go to an appropriate charity. This helps them to feel that some good has come out of their loss, which can be a great comfort.

Self-help

Whatever you think of them, self-help books (classified by the trade as mind, body and spirit) have been ridiculously successful, ever since the genre crashed into public consciousness more than 20 years ago with bestsellers like *The 7 Habits of Highly-Effective People* (Stephen R Covey) and *Men Are From Mars, Women Are From Venus* (John Gray). The first has sold more than 25 million copies (and is still on the best-seller list), the second over 50 million. According to an on-line list published by UK Business Insider (see Appendix II), 10 of the top 20 best-selling books of 2016 so far are basically self-help titles.

It's clear that some people love the comfort and reassurance they get from these books, and sales are helped by the fact that readers of self-help books tend to keep going back for more, even books covering the same ground; we all know people whose shelves are laden with diet books or titles about understanding the inner psyche. The key to success here seems to be finding a truly original approach to your topic, reflected by a real jump-up-and-shout title, like those above. This is not easy, but if you happen to have a real understanding of some life skill which you think others should know about, it could be well worth putting it all down on paper.

Guides and handbooks

Factual books which people will use for reference, such as a guide to an area you know really well, an innovative recipe book or an introduction to a sport in which you're an acknowledged expert, may sell well, and could keep on selling, but they need authority, and what marketing people call *positioning* – that is, your book must have an angle which separates it from the all the other similar ones. For example, if you wrote a guide to walks in the Lake District, why should anyone buy your book instead of those marvellous volumes by Wainwright? You will need the book to be clearly different in some way, perhaps because it is illustrated with quirky pictures, or includes reviews of guesthouses, or it's funny, or it's the first guide of its kind to be small enough to fit into a breast pocket. If you're going to write a cookbook, it may not be enough to market it as 'Joan's Favourite Recipes', or 'My Book of Country Cookery' – it needs to be original or specialist enough to make people sit up and take notice, like a book entirely devoted to the aubergine, or one revealing the 'secrets' of a chef who has cooked for the famous. It's that thing 'positioning' again. As with any supermarket product, nobody will spend good money on a 'how to' book unless they can see the benefits.

Books about stuff

If you have in-depth knowledge of a particular topic – volleyball, stamp-collecting, Mahatma Gandhi, rock-climbing in the Grampians, Neolithic semiotics, property management, Afghanistan, 19th century shipwrecks, the history of the violin, Fleetwood Mac, sundials, self-defence – you may feel inclined to put it all down on paper. If you're a genuine expert on your subject who has already lectured or written about it and has something original to say, there's a good chance that people who share your interest or are studying your subject will buy your book. If you are just another enthusiast, however, by all means go ahead and write your book, but don't expect too many sales, unless it is exceptionally original or entertaining – why would anyone consult your book when they can go to the recognised authorities?

This raises the vital point that to sell a book, you very often first have to sell yourself. More on this later.

Funny books

It is very difficult indeed to write a genuinely funny book. But how can you tell whether yours is up to the mark? Your friends will laugh obediently when you show them extracts, but will your book stack up against the works that sell by the thousand every Christmas from the displays at Waterstones? Many authors think they have written something side-splitting when in truth it is mildly amusing at best, while others rely on gags or situations which will already be familiar to most readers from TV comedy shows, even the school playground; I have just come across a joke in a retired businessman's memoir, presented as new, which I first heard at grammar school several decades ago. Test your material on the market very carefully, and only when you hear the sound of loud, genuine, unsolicited laughter should you put your hopes into a book.

Humour thrives on originality – all the top comics and comic writers have succeeded because they found a new vein, a new way of being funny and jokes which no one had thought of before. That's hard.

'Writing a funny book is so much cheaper than therapy' – Kathy Lette

Children's books

Children's books may seem easy and fun to write, but writing a good one is just as difficult as writing a good story for adults – and it's harder still to make money from a young children's story, because of the high cost of production and the mountain of other books fighting for the same market. If you want to set down in print at your own expense a charming story you've written for your children, that's great, but if you're hoping to sell it, please remember that half the parents, grandparents and aunts in the country have had the same idea, and the competition is fiercer than the Gruffalo.

More about children's books in Chapter 7.

Poetry books

Lots of people write poetry and would like to see their work in a book. That's great, as long as you don't expect the public to buy it. When people buy poetry books they choose the recognised poets, and you can't blame them, because the truth is that the vast majority of 'amateur' verse is really not very good (although I'm sure yours is excellent). Of course, there are no rules about poetry, and as with other works of art, no way of measuring its quality objectively. But as far as sales are concerned, expect a few copies to be picked up by your friends and followers, and that's likely to be it – unless of course you really *are* both talented and original, and people start to talk about your work and recommend it to others.

As with novels, I sometimes wonder if an amateur poet has ever bothered to read the work of the acknowledged greats. It's probably wise to absorb some of the marvellous 'real' poetry that's out there before you have a go yourself.

More about poetry in Chapter 8.

CHAPTER 3

On being good at writing

Given that all of us are born and brought up to learn our native language and practise it every day of our lives from the age of two or three, you'd think we would all be polished practitioners by the time we have left school, yet you need only listen to a conversation in a bus queue or read a longish email from almost anyone to know that this just isn't the case. Those who speak in good English (by which I mean English which is clear, concise and expressive, not necessarily grammatically correct) are in the minority. How often have you listened to an intelligent adult groping unsuccessfully for the right word, or taking three sentences to say what needed only one? Why this should be so is a fascinating question; perhaps most people learn to communicate only as well as they have to, and then don't bother to try to get better at it.

I have noticed that writers whose first language is not English (I have edited many Asian and African authors, in particular) often have excellent English vocabularies but understandably misfire somewhat when it comes to syntax and the more vernacular expressions – hardly surprising, considering how infuriatingly idiomatic and scornful of rules and regularity our language is. They write things like 'since then for a long time' and 'he made me to wait', and tend to omit the definite and indefinite articles, which are not used in their languages the way they are in English (more about this in chapter 13). They tend to use unnecessarily obscure words ('intimate' for 'tell', 'excise' instead of 'cut'), of which they often have a better command than many English people, while we native Anglophones have grown up communicating simply. They also tend to go astray by misusing vernacular phrases; one writer innocently said her domineering schoolteacher had 'had his way with me' – she meant winning an argument. But steady on, don't laugh – could you even begin to write a book in French or Spanish, let alone Gujarati or Hindi?

Overseas authors frequently display an impressive knowledge of our literature, and are surprised to find that most English people don't actually read Dickens, Hardy or even Shakespeare very often.

Fortunately for those of us who do not have the command of English of a Stephen Fry or an Alan Bennett, writing, unlike conversation, does not happen in real time. You can delete, develop, edit, abbreviate, rearrange, correct and check before anyone else gets to read your words – and you must, if you are to produce something worth reading.

Readers make the best writers

'I am always astonished by would-be writers who ask me for advice and admit, quite blithely, that they "don't have time to read". This is like a guy starting up Mount Everest saying he didn't have time to buy any rope or pitons.' – Stephen King

One thing is clear; people who read a lot are much better at writing than those who don't. If you've been soaking up fiction ever since you discovered Enid Blyton when you were seven, you will know instinctively how direct speech works, what internal monologue is (though you may not have realised it was called that) and most important of all, how to tell a story. You will also be able to recognise what's original and what's been done too many times before.

When it comes to writing the book-driven kind of book, most new authors will cheerfully admit that they have no special talent – they just want their baby out there for people to read. That's one reason why they come to a professional editor. 'I'm an engineer, not a writer,' they will say, or 'I was never much good at English at school, you folks can sort all that out for me'. And we editors are very pleased to do so.

With writing-driven books, it's different. Most new writers of fiction take pleasure from the act of writing itself, and would like to learn to do it better. We try to help by pointing out areas where their manuscripts could be improved (most of which are dealt with in this book). One or two of those who take pride in their writing ability get a bit sniffy, but most take our suggestions on board.

Becoming a good writer, and particularly a good novelist, is not an overnight business. If you look into the backgrounds of our most accomplished authors, you'll find that most of them have been reading from the cradle and writing from the kindergarten, and their skill is born of thousands of hours spent at both activities.

The editor's role

Even the finest authors rely on editors, and almost all books need an editor's attention. I once had the privilege of editing an article for a wine publication by the great Roald Dahl, and I can tell you that there were quite a few mistakes in it; it had clearly been hastily written. But Dahl knew what editors were for. His instructions were to edit his text as I saw fit, and that's what I did, though naturally with extreme care. Very, very few writers can match the standard set by Dahl and the rest of that tiny number of happy people who are so good at writing, or so good at inventing stories (or both), that they can do it for a living. Not only that, there is a big difference between writing which has merit and writing which will actually sell, and be well reviewed. Bridging the gulf means talent, plus a lot of hard work.

Don't fool yourself

Most people know whether they are any good at water-skiing or baking Yorkshire puddings. However, just as all men are said to believe they are good drivers, many would-be writers seem quite unaware of their failings when it comes to putting words on paper. Curiously, it's often the authors of the most illiterate manuscripts sent to publishers who claim they have written a best-seller, while many beautifully-crafted books are presented very modestly by authors with few expectations. The less said about some of the manuscripts we have seen at Mereo, the better. Like those hapless contestants in *Britain's Got Talent*, some authors have clearly listened to friends and relations who have assured them that they are going to be a star and their book is the best thing since the last John Grisham. Some people are still impressed by the simple fact that someone they know has actually written a book, as opposed to a note to the milkman – never mind if it is readable, the marvel is that it was written at all.

Unfortunately people close to you won't tell you the truth, even if they know it. It's one thing to tell your friend that the dress she's about to buy doesn't suit her; it's quite another to say that the book she has been slaving over for the past three years has dozens of spelling mistakes, along with a ridiculous ending and a plot with a hole in it. So people don't say such things.

It's different when you send a book to a reputable self-publisher. Having taken a look at your book, they will diplomatically let you know if it is not publishable without further work at your end, and what that work should be (there will usually be a charge for a detailed review). If the basics are there, the editor will work with the author to turn it into a polished book.

Having said all that, many of the better self-published books are as good as anything on the bookshop shelves and deserve to do well.

'If it sounds like writing, I rewrite it.' – Elmore Leonard

So what's the difference between good writing and bad?

By 'good writing' I mean prose which sweeps the reader into the story, which paints enticing pictures in her mind, which makes her long to know what happens next. I mean writing which makes the reader care about the story, the characters, the ending. Good writing delivers its message and then gets out of the way. It is often invisible; it doesn't make you think 'gosh, that was a clever metaphor' or 'what a beautifully-crafted sentence', it just drives you to read on, and keep reading on, until the story is finished. And then to start again, or grab another book by the same author.

'The height of storytelling – oral or written – is when the teller becomes invisible.' – Aaron Shepard, children's author

Write and rewrite

Nobody writes a publishable manuscript in one go, particularly with fiction (where you can change the story as well as the way you tell it). Book-driven authors often work on an MS until it's complete, give it the once-over and then pass it to an editor. That's fine by us. Writing-driven authors are more likely to go over an MS a number of times to polish up the style and the English. By all accounts published novelists push themselves the hardest, writing, rewriting, deleting, recasting, renaming and restructuring until the book is as good as they can make it.

As a beginner, you are well advised to follow that example. If you know what good writing looks like, you should be able to apply that knowledge to critique your own work, looking for ways of streamlining sentences, improving narrative sequence, replacing clichés with original expressions, pruning adjectives and adverbs and checking you've made the best choices from your vocabulary. When you've done all that, leave the whole thing in a drawer for a week and then go back to it; with fresh eyes, you'll see ways of improving it that had never occurred to you before, and in particular you'll notice repetition – where you have given the same information twice, or used the same word twice within a few lines.

"The first draft is just you telling yourself the story." — *Terry Pratchett*

Understanding sentences and paragraphs

Some authors divide their text into sentences which are all about the same length; although I suspect they do not realise it, this makes for a very tedious read. Far better to vary your sentences, from one-word exclamations all the way through to monsters of a hundred words or more. It seems to me that it's one of the hallmarks of a good writer to be able to do this.

Jake did a quick run-through of women in his mind, not of the ones he had known or dealt with in the past few months of years so much as all of them: their concern with the surface of things, with objects and appearances, with their surroundings and how they looked and sounded in them, with seeming to be better and to be right while getting everything wrong, their automatic assumption of the role of injured party in any clash of wills, their certainty that a view is the more credible and useful for the fact that they hold it, their use of misunderstanding and misrepresentation as weapons of debate, their selective sensitivity to tones of voice, their unawareness of the difference in themselves between sincerity

and insincerity, their interest in importance (together with noticeable inability to discriminate in that sphere), their fondness for general conversation and directionless discussion, their pre-emption of the major share of feeling, their exaggerated estimate of their own plausibility, their never listening and lots of other things like that, all according to him.
– Jake's Thing, *Kingsley Amis*

On the face of it that 178-word sentence is hopelessly long (and I'm not recommending you try to copy Amis), yet it knows exactly where it's going. Amis was a writer from an age when literary excellence was valued more than it is today. If I sound nostalgic, I am, a little.

So make sure you use a few short, punchy sentences among the longer ones, particularly at the beginnings and ends of paragraphs, while avoiding anything that is so long it loses its way and leaves the reader gasping for breath.

Write in **paragraphs** – real paragraphs, not just arbitrary carriage returns chucked in every few lines. Paragraph breaks are not metric units of text (five sentences make one paragraph, 50 paragraphs make one chapter) but a feature of good writing. A new paragraph is suggested when there is a slight change of subject, argument or point of view, or a jump in time or place. Imagine the scene you're describing is being filmed. When the camera cuts to a different view or angle, that's often the equivalent of a new paragraph.

There is no rule about how long a paragraph should be, but very long paragraphs (only two or three per page) will make the text indigestible and very short ones (20-30 words) create a jumpy, staccato effect (unless they are required by the conventions of handling direct speech), so both are to be avoided.

One common mistake is to imagine that each item under a category should have a new paragraph – for example if the writer is itemising his subject's three children he gives each a brief new paragraph, although in truth this is only appropriate if each child is being described in some detail (that may come later).

A few novice authors write in a stream-of-consciousness style which defies the very idea of paragraphing. Simply using the return key every few lines will not help, because there are no natural breaks. Reading an MS like this is like drinking from a hosepipe. It is very difficult indeed for an editor to rescue this kind of prose.

With new sentences and paragraph breaks, it helps to imagine reading the text aloud to an audience. Where would you pause for a couple of seconds? Where would you let your voice rise or fall? Where would you speed up or slow down? This will help you to decide where the paragraph breaks should be, and when a new sentence is required.

When there is a jump in time or a change of scene, a good technique is to use a line break (an extra space) to indicate that there's a natural break in the story. You can stick a row of asterisks in if you like, to mark a division which does not quite merit a new chapter.

Getting help

'You can't teach someone to know how to use words effectively and beautifully. You can help people who can write to write more effectively and you can probably teach people a lot of little tips for writing a novel, but I don't think somebody who cannot write and does not care for words can ever be made into a writer. It just is not possible.' – P D James

I'm with P D James on this. Not everyone has an ear for good, compelling prose, and no rulebook will enable you to write it. But if you have ability which needs developing, there is help out there; there are books, websites, clubs and learning institutions devoted to helping writers with some innate ability to do their stuff better. According to *The Guardian*, more than 90 British universities now offer postgraduate degrees in writing and there are 10,000 short creative writing courses available in the UK (the Writers' and Artists' Yearbook lists many, see 'Where to find out more' at the back of this book). I would only suggest that you make sure you take advice from someone who is either a publishing professional or an experienced published writer, rather than rely on tutors whose knowledge is mainly academic.

CHAPTER 4

How not to write an autobiography or biography

When you're writing about your own life (or indeed about someone else's), planning is not quite as challenging as it is with a novel, because it's natural to write in chronological order, and as the story is already in your head you don't need to invent it (I hope). Nevertheless, it makes sense to decide which areas you will cover and which you won't. An encyclopaedic autobiography, dealing equally with childhood, schooling, love and marriage, career, leisure activities, holidays, medical issues and so on and running through the years all the way from how your parents met to what you were doing yesterday, is likely to be rather long, and dare I say it, rather boring. The most readable autobiographies are those that focus on just one of these aspects; your childhood in India, for example, your army service, or your career as an athlete. The rest can be brief, but it should be there, so that readers understand where you came from and where you ended up. If they develop an interest in you through reading your book, as they should, they will wonder about you, your background, your family and what you got up to when you were not fighting boardroom battles/sailing round the world/campaigning for human rights. So try to identify a theme to your life, and make that the main focus.

Here are some of the essentials:

Know who you're writing for. You should always be writing for one imaginary reader, never as if you were addressing an audience. It will help to be clear in your mind who he or she is; someone just like you? A middle-aged housewife? A university graduate? A former colleague? Your grandson?

Whatever sort of book you're writing, please don't address your readers plurally by using terms like 'those of you'. It will make you sound like a lecturer and will irritate your readers.

Use the right tone. Just as some people talk quite naturally until they are asked to give an after-dinner speech, some write quite naturally until they adopt the role of author. They produce stilted, pompous or too-clever-by-half prose which will give most readers indigestion within a few lines. So take it easy. Avoid the temptation to sound important or clever (however clever or important you actually are), to take yourself too seriously or to show off your literary skills. If in doubt, simply get your thoughts down using the natural language that first comes into your head. Then work through it, reconstructing your sentences and sharpening the text into good English.

Incidentally, never apologise to your readers for your book

before they have read it, at least not if you're hoping to sell it. You wouldn't believe how many factual manuscripts begin 'I'm not much of a writer' or 'May I apologise in advance if this book rambles on a bit…' You might as well tell them to throw the book away now.

Simplify your story. The fact is, our lives are not stories. They are 75 or 80 years (if you're lucky) of stuff, of staggering from place to place, of plans and prospects punctuated (and maybe punctured) by random events good and bad. Life is contingent, and you are rarely if ever in full control of it; sometimes you are not in control at all. So if you want to make a story of your life, you need to be somewhat ruthless in weeding out most of the irrelevant, the accidental, the boring. Otherwise your book will just be a brain dump on paper.

Real life involves many side turnings, blind alleys and random experiences which have no bearing on anything else. Some of these will be useful as background, to build a picture of the world you lived in and your own character, but if they don't do this, leave them out (funny stories are fine).

Plan and write your story in **chronological order**, at least initially. Start at the beginning and finish at the end, dealing as thoroughly as you can with one episode before moving onto the next. Any other approach will cause confusion for you in later revision, for your editor and eventually for your readers. It will also make it very easy to leave things out. Once you have a completed MS you can start thinking about subtle devices such as starting the story with a key passage from the middle (a prologue – see Chapter 5) before going back to origins.

If there are two or three threads to your story – your career, home life and sporting success, for example – some relaxing of this rule will be necessary to avoid constantly switching between subjects. So you might devote a chapter or two to your first job, for example, followed by one on how you got to play tennis for your county, then on to a section about meeting your partner and getting married, before returning to how you left your job and set up your own business.

Vary the pace. If you tell your story at the same speed all the way through, you will soon send the reader to sleep. Speed your way over the incidentals ('After three more weeks of dawn starts and greasy breakfasts I had had enough…' but then slow right down to deal with the key moments − 'He turned, one hand fingering the knife. I took a step back. My throat was dry. Somewhere in the distance, a bell rang…'

Avoid too much **repetition**. If you're describing events which happened several times in your life − starting a new job, winning a sporting event, hospital treatment − it gets tedious if you describe each one with the same level of detail. Focus on the first time or one of the key ones, then gloss over the rest.

How to use chapters

The first rule about chapters is not to have too many of them. Some authors like to begin a new chapter on every other page, which breaks the book up and makes it very scrappy. Around 8-20 chapters is about right for most books. But it's not just a question of length − it's about the way you use your chapters. Authors often tend to follow the one subject, one chapter rule (one about Hong Kong, one about Hampshire, one about hang-gliding), but this falls apart when you have only a page or two to say on one topic and 40 pages about another, and in any case a good book should maintain a continuous, linked narrative, rather than consisting of a series of disjointed essays on separate subjects.

It feels tidy to end a chapter when you've finished with a particular topic and then start the next with a new one, so all your chapters are boxed off from each other and could be read in a different order. But this is a mistake, because if you do that you are no longer telling a story and there's nothing to keep the reader reading. It is much more satisfactory to end each chapter with a hint of what is to come: 'As I said farewell to Mary on the platform that day, I felt a deep sense of loss and sadness, believing I would never see her again. Little did I know how events would turn out'.

So in planning your chapters, have a think about how they could be linked together, with some overlaps in narrative. Let's imagine you served with the army and were posted from the Rhine to Northern Ireland. Many an author would start the Ulster chapter 'In May 1972 my CO called me in and told me I was being posted to Ulster'. How much better it would be if instead you wrote at the end of the Rhine chapter: 'With great mates like Johnny and weekends skiing with Gretchen in Innsbrück, I was beginning to feel settled at last. And then on the Sunday morning the CO called me in and told me to pack my kit. They wanted me on the Tuesday flight to Belfast'. Belfast – aaargh! Immediately the reader has a reason to read on.

Will anybody read it?

If you're writing simply to transfer your own memories to paper – a curiously satisfying pursuit – then how you tackle your book and what you put in it is entirely up to you. However, if you're writing in the hope that anyone will read your book – and I mean anyone, including your immediate family – you really ought to try to make it interesting and enjoyable.

So how do you do that?

I think you might start by remembering that even those who love you dearly may not want to sit down and read a 150,000-word account of your life, taking in every boardroom battle, every round of golf, every holiday in the Seychelles. They are much more likely to dip into it, look up particular episodes and key characters (an index will be helpful for this, see chapter 13) and read the bits which happen to be about them. People who are mere acquaintances may gracefully receive the book as a gift (very likely they will equally gracefully insist on paying for their copy), but actually reading it is likely to be one of those jobs they never quite get round to, like sorting out the CD collection or tidying the garden shed. After all, it will take them considerably longer than either.

'A successful book is not made of what is in it, but what is left out of it.' – Mark Twain

Who are you going to be?

The best factual first-person books are those in which the writer has consciously defined a character for himself or herself and sticks to it, almost as if writing a first-person novel. This is a subtle point, but an important one. It means that before you start writing you should ask yourself who you are writing *as.* Are you going to present yourself as a carefree, imperturbable sort, like Michael J 'Crocodile' Dundee in the films, or a grumpy Victor Meldrew with a caustic (but funny) comment about everything? Do you want to come across as an innocent or a sage? Do you want to sound bouncy and engaged, like Bill Oddie, or cool and detached, like Alan Whicker? Several shades of personality lurk within all of us, and we subconsciously adopt and adapt them to suit the situations we find ourselves in and the people we meet. You want the reader to like you, after all.

The multi-million-selling travel writer Bill Bryson gets this just right, always sounding cheerful, philosophical and uncomplaining in the face of all manner of frustrations and disappointments. Even when he is excoriating the US news media for dumbing down or deriding the relentless domination of fast food outlets, he uses cool facts to make his point, never sounding angry or bad-tempered. I don't know whether Bryson is as congenial in the flesh as he is in print (though I rather suspect he is), but whether he is or not, he manages to maintain a consistent tone in his writings. Their warmth, likeability and humour are a large part of what makes them so successful.

Making them read on

The events of your life are a matter of fact and no invention will be required (I hope), but you still have to tell your story so that people will read it. You still have to make the reader care about you and the people in your life, so that they want to turn the page to find out whether Lucinda said yes to your proposal, or if you went through with the move to Canada.

If you want your book to be a good read and to appeal to strangers, the first thing you should do is to take out most of the stuff about the humdrum stages of your life entirely, as mentioned above, and focus on the central adventure – your years in the limelight as a singer, your battle with depression, your army career, your imprisonment by the Japanese, your part in the development of the Large Hadron Collider. The late Sir Fred Hoyle, a great and pioneering cosmologist, wrote a dozen best-selling science fiction novels, but he didn't even mention them in his autobiography *Home Is Where The Wind Blows*, presumably because he wanted to be remembered for his work. There's no doubt that selective autobiographies are likely to make for a much better read than the cradle-to-grave jobs, if readers are what you're after.

True-life adventures

Taking the above principle to its logical extreme, your book might be about a single episode in your life, covering quite a short period. *The Journey That Never Was* by Jeanne de Ferranti (Mereo, 2015) relates how two young women drove around the world in a factory-standard Mini, way back in 1961. This remarkable trip was hushed up by her parents and never revealed to the world, and the story was not told until Jeanne came to Mereo with a book about it, more than half a century later. The action in Joe Simpson's *Touching the Void* (1988), the electrifying story of how Simpson survived the aftermath of a climbing accident after his companion had been forced to cut the rope that connected them, covers the events of just three days.

Here's Bill Bryson leading us into temptation with the first sentence of one of his most absorbing books:

Not long after I moved with my family to a small town in New Hampshire, I happened upon a path that vanished into a wood on the edge of town. – A Walk In The Woods, *Bill Bryson (Black Swan, 1997)*

A vanishing path? Tell me more! That phrase has echoes of the most compelling stories of childhood. The rest of the book is about Bryson's attempt to hike the 2200-mile Appalachian Trail. Where does the vanishing path vanish to? (The other end of America.) Will Bill get lost? (Yes.) Will his amiable but somewhat dissolute companion be able to stand the pace? (No.) Will their friendship survive? Is that a bear outside the tent? We want to know.

Writing about success

'I met President Kennedy only twice…'

Writing about a life of success and comfortable living is much more difficult than writing about adversity and suffering, because it is so hard to avoid sounding smug and self-satisfied. That's why the first half of the average celebrity memoir is so much better to read than the second (take Kirk Douglas' *The Ragman's Son* – the first part is a moving account of survival on the mean streets, while the anticlimactic second part is a gushing catalogue of encounters with the people Douglas got to know when he became rich and famous).

So if you have had a successful life and everything has gone pretty well for the last seventy years or whatever, barring the odd parking ticket or bout of toothache, you need to find ways of keeping the reader on your side and do your best not to sound pleased with yourself. I suggest you play up the adversity and the conflict, and particularly the humour, and pass relatively briefly over the triumphs. It's difficult to tell readers about great successes without sounding unpleasantly smug. Don't be tempted to resort to false modesty, which is even more annoying ('I was surprised to get a standing ovation, and you could have knocked me down with a feather when the chairman gave me the Caribbean job'). Perhaps it is best not to tell your readers this sort of thing, however closely related they are to you, if you don't want them to throw the book aside in disgust. They will soon work out from your story that you were good at your job. You could always list your achievements soberly in an appendix, like a CV. But bear in mind that everyone who is likely to read your book will already know that you were chairman of International Staples at the age of 42. Or whatever.

So go easy on the achievement, and when you do report it, do it straight – 'the following week they asked me to stand as MP', not 'It was with astonishment and great humility...' etc. Focus on the world around you and the personalities of those in it, rather than your own. If you have a sense of humour, it will help enormously. Humour, particularly if it's at your own expense, is a great antidote to smugness.

Stick to the story

Real life is messy, and it's invariably packed with side turnings, blind alleys and random experiences which have no bearing on anything else. So in telling your story, don't allow yourself to be distracted by the trivia, the tales which may have gone down well over the years around the barbecue but will just drag your story down if there are too many of them.

You can't stay too chronological. If there are two or three

threads to your story, as there are with most of us – your career, home life and sporting success, for example – you might devote a chapter or two to your first job, followed by one on how you got to play tennis for your county, then on to a section about meeting your partner and getting married, before returning to how you left your job and set up your own business. If you keep to a strict timeline, you're going to be darting back and forth between boardroom and sitting room every other page. However for planning purposes, it's wise to set out a timeline and list on it all the events you want to include.

Similarly, keep to the central theme of your book. If your story is about how you spent ten years with nomads in Siberia, don't tell us all about your tour of the sights of Europe on the way home – it will just come across as an anti-climax.

The diary approach

If your book is about your day-to-day life as say a publican, a district nurse or a wartime sailor, the diary approach can work well. Even if you didn't keep a diary at the time, you may be able to reconstruct one, if your memory is good enough. The drawback of many diaries is that they become boring and repetitive, because most days of most people's lives are boring and repetitive when retold, even if some were anything but. So you will have to prune ruthlessly, including dull passages only to provide contrast to the excitement.

1916, March 30th – Had a stroll around the village. The people have no idea of sanitation or cleanliness and live crowded in little mud huts into which the cattle, fowls etc. go.

I shouldn't think the natives ever wash themselves.

April 8th – There was a heavy thunderstorm in the night and it is raining now.

April 10th – Heard that the SS Simba has been sunk with the mail.

April 13th – Played hockey for Signals.

April 16th – Church parade. Teddy Graske shot himself through the head. I heard the rifle go off and rushed into his room to see what was up and found him on the floor with the rifle under him.

From *The Messenger*, the World War I diary of Oswald Early, Wireless Operator, by Russell Early (Mereo, 2014)

Description

When describing a scene from your past, try to add that telling detail that will bring it to life. You can use shorthand terms like 'jungle', 'slum' or '1970s housing estate', leaving it to the reader to colour in a rough outline. But then you need to say what's special about your jungle, your slum or your housing estate.

Here is a woman's description of revisiting her childhood home back in England – using Google Earth – in middle age:

They have painted the pebble-dash white and the bricks redder than they were, and within the porch, a lasting, sensible structure of brick, there is a white door where once – oh so long ago – there was a green door with a round window in it. The windows upstairs and down no longer open like a book but with a flap, in the top part only. The little front garden with two round bushes and a hedge and roses is all gone, concreted over so that the owner can drive his car off the road and park it under his own window, deeming this to be a better view than a bit of green. There are vertical blinds at the windows to stop people looking in, and perhaps the owner never looks out anyway; what would there be to see?

Through the Gate, *Jean Meyer (Mereo 2015)*

As that author found, Google Earth will show you exactly what all kinds of places look like, from mountains and beaches to hotels, high streets and housing estates (though as she discovered, they may have changed since your time).

Where a setting plays a vital role in a book – the place where your subject wrote his poetry, for example – you need to do your best to put the reader there. This was my description of the writer and broadcaster Hugh Falkus' home for 40 years:

Cragg Cottage sits grey and foursquare in a corner of the lower north-western slopes of Birkby Fell, the granite stump of Raven Crag at its back, Eskdale spread out before it. Even today, when you stand in the lane by the cottage and survey the valley, no other building is in sight. The landscape is a muted weave of birch woodland and cultivated pine plantations, tussocky bog and green pasture, rocky prominences and centuries-old stone walls. Walk up past Cragg Farm on to the slopes of Raven Crag and the blue thread of Hugh's river appears in the middle distance, winding and widening as it passes Muncaster Castle on its way down to Ravenglass and the Irish Sea. – A Life on the Edge, *Medlar Press, 2007*

Names and places

The people in your story are central to your book, so you need to describe them properly. Introduce them at the right point. Explain who someone is the first time you mention them, and then do not repeat it. Full names and titles need be given only once; after that Dr Andrew Harbottle becomes Andrew or Dr Harbottle, unless he is being reintroduced after a long interval.

Try to avoid bringing in lots of people and places whose roles in your story are too minor to merit proper description. A little simplification makes for a much better read; if you were a musician, you don't need to deal faithfully with every gig you played or every drummer you worked with, just as, when telling of a journey, you don't need to describe all the towns you went through, just the interesting ones.

Authors often give the name of a character once, then demote them to a 'he' or 'she' ever after. It's good style to remind the reader of the name of the central character in your 'scene' at intervals, eg at the beginning of a new paragraph, instead of endlessly repeating '*he* said…' or '*she* turned…', particularly if it isn't absolutely clear any longer who we are talking about. Never make your reader stop and scratch his head over who's doing what with whom.

Give all your characters names (false ones if necessary), if they feature more than once. It may seem obvious, but we see many manuscripts in which 'Mike's sister' or 'the friend' are referred to repeatedly without being given names – very clumsy. But see above – don't overload your narrative with people just for the sake of completeness. Novels shouldn't have too many characters, and nor should a true-life story if you want it to be a good read.

Naming names

Publishers are often asked if an author can write freely about other people and their doings in a true-life story without getting into trouble. This caution applies to the names of companies and organisations too; it's very common to see references to 'a famous animal charity' or 'a national supermarket'. This is irritating; why not name them? There's nothing to stop you mentioning real people and organisations without their blessing – journalists do it for a living every day of the week (I should know, I was one). From the legal point of view, you should have nothing to worry about as long as you don't risk contravening the laws of defamation, professional confidentiality and state secrecy. Talking of which:

Don't risk libel

If you have said unkind things about living people who can be identified in your book, the simple fact of publication, even if no one actually buys it, could lay you open to accusations of libel, and you really don't want that (nor for that matter does your publisher). Libel can be claimed when you make a damaging statement about a living person – something which could be said to harm their reputation – or repeat such a damaging statement made by someone else. You may be quite certain it's true, but what if you can't prove it? And what will it cost to do so, in the awful event of a libel suit?

You might get away with insulting people with statements of opinion – 'I found Frank Frink a pompous buffoon' – but not with making damaging factual allegations ('Frank Frink was incompetent/cooking the books/having an affair with his secretary').

I suggest that the safest course is to assume that anything you say about a person in your book may get back to that person or their friends and relations, and consider whether they might feel offended, compromised or embarrassed. The only way to avoid trouble is not to make such statements, or if you must, to disguise the identity of the person – not just by giving them a new name but by changing or removing any other information in the book by which they could be identified to anyone; if the person's wife can tell it's her husband you're writing about, that's enough.

This can be tricky if the person had a close association with you. For example, if you say your business partner was on the fiddle, or your first husband defrauded his employer, changing his name will be no use, because his identity will be given away by his association with you. In that situation you'd have to change your own name and publish under a pseudonym – tricky, and possibly pointless.

Organisations can be libelled too, though generally to win damages they will have to prove they have suffered substantial financial loss as a result of what you wrote. Again, identification is critical. If you describe a hotel and its real-life location but change its name, it could still claim you had identified it, so you'd have to go further and disguise it in other ways.

Your subject can't sue you for libel if he's dead, but you can still get into trouble with his nearest and dearest. Those left behind will be pretty annoyed if you claim (without good evidence) that their late loved one was a fraudster, or the secret father of a famous pop star. As I write this, the family of the late Poet Laureate Ted Hughes is furiously demanding changes to a new biography which reports among other things, that they 'stopped for a good lunch' while taking his body from London to Devon for cremation and left mourners standing in the rain after the ceremony.

Sometimes an author has a grudge against someone, legitimate or otherwise, and sets out to expose their evil doings in a book. Don't expect a publisher to agree to this, because however justified your allegations are, it could involve the firm (and you) in expensive legal action.

Skip the history lesson

Your reminiscences of life half a century or more ago will be well worth sharing with your readers, but do give them a personal perspective, an element of originality. If you want to explain, for example, post-war rationing, don't give your readers a tutorial about it (they can Google it if they want to know the details). Much better to tell us how your sisters squabbled over the oranges or your uncle sold clothing coupons on the black market.

The same applies to the events of history. We don't need to hear all about the Normandy landings again unless you were there and can give us an eyewitness account, as opposed to the one we've all heard from TV documentaries. Nor do we need to be told about the assassination of President Kennedy or the moon landings (unless, again, you were there); everyone over the age of 60 has their own perfectly good memory of those. Of course, if you are writing for a younger audience such as your grandchildren, you may feel a light-hearted history lesson would be a great idea.

Wikipedia is a peerless source of information for writers (I make a monthly donation out of sheer guilt, and hope you do too if you use it a lot), but many factual books are let down by what I think of as 'wikidumps' – chunks of material lifted from the Net and reworded for the reader, such as a brief history of comprehensive education or the vital statistics of Ecuador. A passage like this is so obviously not from the author's own knowledge that in the average autobiography it's as incongruous as a fish finger in a bouillabaisse.

It's not unusual for an otherwise interesting, even inspiring memoir, to end on a sour note with a rant about the standard gripes of the seventh age – ghastly commercialism, the youth of today, corruption in sport, declining public services and so on. Much better to leave your readers on a positive note. And please don't keep reminding us that there were 'no mobiles in those days'.

Wish you weren't here

'There was a time when a book could be sold purely because its author had been to distant climes and had returned to tell of the exotic sights he had seen. That author was Marco Polo, and the time was the thirteenth century.' – Sandra Newman & Howard Mittelmark, How Not To Write A Novel

If you're old enough to remember the days when Uncle Harold and Aunty Beryl would invite the family round to an evening of cocktail sausages and Spanish plonk and then clunk-click their helpless captives through 500 slides of their holiday in Torremolinos, you will understand why you should give as little space as possible in your book to your holiday experiences. Conventional holidays are plain boring when related second hand, while it can be quite sick-making to have to listen to your wealthier friends' tales of an adventure cruise to Patagonia or Antarctica.

As with historical events, the key is to have something original to say, so you don't sound like a holiday brochure. Try to make light of the herds of wildebeest, the 17 kinds of fruit served at breakfast on the beach, the amazing service at your five-star hotel. Instead, go a little deeper. Try to focus on the unusual, even the disastrous. Tell your reader about the culture, the shameful poverty, the religious extremism, the topical, the political, the interesting. If you met George Clooney in a bar or discovered a new species of frog, great. And if it went horribly wrong because you got mugged or the coach crashed, let's have all the details. Your readers will love it.

Finding a title

If your book is going on sale, it's going to need a strong, original title, and preferably a unique one (check if it's been used by looking on Amazon). It needs to be intriguing, and to carry a strong image.

Some factual books practically title themselves; others, those which lack a central theme, are more challenging. If your book is about how you went around the world on water-skis, you may not need to look much further than 'Water-Skiing Round the World'. If it's about a life spent in a variety of places doing several different jobs, it may not be so easy.

If you have commercial ambitions for your book, the title needs to be as striking, compelling and original as possible. It does not need to be factually balanced in the way a report title would have to be, contrary to the assumption of many. Authors often come up with titles which are hobbled by this notion; we suggest 'A Life in Medicine' and in the pursuit of accuracy they come back with 'A Life in Medicine, Medical Research and Postgraduate Teaching'. Would you read it? Neither would I.

Other titles just try to squeeze in too much information (I made these examples up, by the way):

Working as an engineer in Pakistan, India and Bangladesh (suggested: *Dams and Dynamite*)

Abandoned Farmsteads, Old Vineyards and Italian Villages (suggested: *A Small House in Tuscany*)

From Philadelphia's Fields to Virginia's Vineyards (suggested: *American Sunrise*)

Your title should focus on one central idea, not a whole bunch of them, and be no more than half a dozen words (unless its strength relies on an attention-grabbing statement, like *Men Are From Mars, Women Are From Venus* – interestingly, many of the most successful self-help books have very long titles) and preferably one, two or three; one-word titles are very popular these days, at least with fiction, but it needs to be a damn good word (*Lolita, Atonement*). They should also be distinctive, so that the book can be found and identified easily on the internet. We very often have to break the news to an author right at the beginning that his title won't do, because there are already four or five books out there with the same one, or almost the same. 'But there's no copyright on titles!' he will point out, correctly. No, but sharing a title with other books can make internet marketing (which is the main kind of book marketing, these days) tricky, and is best avoided, particularly if another book with your title has recently been published in a similar genre.

Totally straight, descriptive titles ('An Introduction to Sudoku') may be OK for purely factual books, as long as the subject itself is reasonably original; if there are lots of books about Sudoku out there (which there are) you're going to need something more interesting – 'Sudoku for Sleepwalkers' or 'How To Be a Sudoku Addict and Stay Married'). It's that thing 'positioning' again. For an autobiography, 'My Life At Sea' would be a plain, boring title for what the reader will assume is a plain, boring book. 'Herrings and Hurricanes' would be better. Double meanings work very well ('Stormy Waters').

Some of the best titles are too good to be true, because they have been used many times before:

Flying High
The Time of my Life
As it Seemed to Me

Many good titles have a metaphorical quality, while others use a play on words of some kind:

Tall, Dark and Gruesome
Christopher Lee

Look Back in Hunger
Jo Brand

My Family and Other Animals
Gerald Durrell

One useful dodge is to start with a familiar phrase and then try replacing one word (you can do this in the text too):

Once Upon a Horse
And the Rest was Geography

At Mereo we try to come up with titles which capture the essence of a book as pithily as possible:

The Butterfly's Cage (Shahnaz Khan)
The story of a young Pakistani woman who was abused and imprisoned by her family for rejecting her psychopathic fiancé.

The Crocodile's Teeth (Sam Thaker)
The story of a man terrorised by Idi Amin's thugs in 1970s Uganda.

Sometimes a telling phrase in the text lends itself to a good title:

A Quiet Authority (Alan Gaunt)
A portrait of the author's soldier father.

Up the Creek Without a Tadpole (Gillian Griffith)
A moving account of living with a parent with Alzheimer's, the title taken from a phrase the victim used.

The title is usually followed by a short subtitle which expands upon it by encapsulating what the book is about:

Apple Pie Beds
An affectionate memoir of boarding school life
(Diane Langdon)

The Promise I Kept
A mother's journey to save a child from the poverty and
squalor of post-Cold War Romania (Adele Rickerby)

Will your autobiography sell?

It's not unusual for authors to start out by saying their book is for family and friends only, and then decide later in the process that actually, they would quite like it to be put on sale, just in case (they say with a modest smile) anyone out there might want to buy it. That's fine, but please be realistic. However good your book is, people who don't know you have rather a lot of choice; there are thousands of autobiographies out there already about people they don't know. Why should they pick yours?

Suppose you founded a building company which went on to become quite large and has now been passed on to your offspring. It will be a story of success, with a few setbacks along the way. There will be a lot of stuff about the challenges of the early days, the difficulties you encountered and how you overcame them. It ought to be a good read, you think. But who will actually read it? Your family, presumably; your colleagues, present and former; other building company owners, particularly those in your area. Some of these people will expect to be given a copy. Others will be interested in looking at the book, but aren't much into reading and hardly ever buy books, even about things that interest them. You might end up giving away 20-30 copies and selling perhaps 50 or 100 – if you're lucky.

Now suppose you were the MD of a company that got involved some years ago in a Government defence contract which went horribly wrong, with allegations in the newspapers of corruption, industrial espionage, maybe a death in suspicious circumstances. If you feel able to tell the story (see page 49 for a discussion of the risks of libel), you have a much better chance of selling it – IF it is revelatory, IF it tells the world stuff the papers would have seized upon if they had known. This one could sell in good numbers, given correct promotion.

The key difference between these two scenarios is that the second book is a commercial product, and should be treated as such. The story will have to be focused – most readers will not be very interested in your family history, your hobbies and what you're doing in retirement, they'll want to cut to the chase. So you'll need to keep it to the matter in hand.

Damaged lives

My firm has published quite a few personal accounts about dealing with the major trials of life – chronic disease, disability, abuse, deprivation. They are usually written with two aims – to explain to the world what it's like to be, for example, deaf, in the interests of achieving more understanding for similarly afflicted people, and to help the author turn what has happened to them into something positive. These are great motives for writing a book, and indeed such books have been among the most moving and inspiring of those we have published. Curiously, most of them are written by women. Perhaps we men like to deal with such matters in a different way.

What often impresses me is the 'shrug your shoulders and get on with it' attitude that many such authors display. They don't moan or grumble or talk about unfairness – at least not once they've got over the first diagnosis. They learn to appreciate life more fully than before, and take delight in the things they can still do.

'Writing has helped so much. I feel as if the storm has lifted, and I can see the way to a clearer horizon. It has all been worthwhile. Life still has much to offer.' – Janet Julings, A Day in a Life (*Mereo, 2012*), the story of a wife and mother struck down by multiple sclerosis

Often these books are surprisingly entertaining, as well as uplifting and revealing. A woman's account of the impossible challenges of dealing with her demented mother; a cancer sufferer's battle with the malignant brain cancer she christened 'Tallulah the Tumour'; a deaf woman's story of battling officials who seemed incapable of learning how to communicate with her.

That's a valuable lesson for anyone writing a story about personal adversity – always approach your story with a positive attitude. Life stories which read like one long grumble against injustice and ill fortune (however justified) will attract few readers. Focus on the humour, the achievements (without boasting too much), the good friends you made, how you won through against adversity in the end.

In loving memory

The pain of bereavement is not something that goes away; you just have to learn to live with it. And people do, in different ways and to different degrees. Our authors have told us how much writing a book in memory of the one they lost has helped them.

Such books are not usually written primarily to sell, and when people do buy them, the proceeds tend to be directed to an appropriate charity.

'They say its gets easier, but it doesn't – you just get used to feeling incomplete. I lost my son, my best friend. But still life goes on.' – Micheline Scarlett, author of I'm Still Here Mum *(Mereo, 2015)*

A book about someone who has gone is so deeply personal that most authors will not need much advice about what to say. It will be one person's story, from first breath to last, a detailed account of a life that is now over, perhaps in the first flush of youth, perhaps in advanced age. Vivid detail will help a great deal – remembered conversations, adventures and escapades, funny sayings, triumphs and disasters.

I would counsel against too much direct description of grief. The most moving books of this kind are those where the events speak for themselves. There's a saying among actors 'If you cry, the audience won't', and I think it applies to books too. Bravery and self-control are far moving than uncontrolled grief.

Self-published biographical books about people who have died tend to be quite short, and often need developing a little. It will help to invite others who knew the subject to contribute their own stories and anecdotes. It's best to give them some guidance – not 'write what you like', as they may send something that's impractically long or inappropriate, and you don't want to have to go back and tell them their piece can't be used or has to be changed. Ask for say, 200-500 words and point out that it may need to be edited (it almost certainly will).

Writing someone else's story

If you're setting out to write a biography, most of the above guidelines still apply. You'll need to be clear at the beginning why you are writing the book. Is it because the subject wants you to write it (or would have wanted you to if he/she had still been around)? If so, you are in effect writing someone else's autobiography for them, and you will want to include what they would want to include and leave out what they would want left out.

If on the other hand the book is your idea and you're writing it because you have a particular interest in your subject or feel their life will make a good and marketable story, you're in the driving seat. You should, however, bear in mind the likely feelings and wishes of the subject's nearest and dearest. Many people's lives are interesting in ways they do not want anyone to know about (or if they have passed on, their friends and relations want to protect their reputation). When I wrote a biography of the late wildlife film-maker, writer and angling wizard Hugh Falkus, I was lucky enough to be given free rein by his family to tell his colourful and somewhat scandalous story warts and all. A fellow writer I know was less fortunate in his work about an equally famous figure, because the man's wife was still around to stand guard over his reputation and make sure the truth did not come out.

If you're writing the book for yourself, you're going to need to operate like an investigative journalist, questioning, challenging, probing, digging, corroborating. Don't be tempted to rely on a few friendly sources; they may be protecting your subject's reputation, and however close they were/are to him, they won't know everything. Pursue everyone who may have something fresh to add, whether close friends or distant acquaintances, colleagues or family, allies or enemies. And *interview* them; don't just chat to them. Record the interviews if possible, and always take notes. Get the detail; when you're told that your man once had a stand-up row with Tony Blair in the House of Commons restaurant you want to know everything that was said, the food on the table, eye-witness accounts, any little piece of colour you can add to make that key scene come to life. To achieve this you may well have to push your interviewees diplomatically beyond the bounds of polite conversation, something many non-journalists, understandably, are reluctant to do.

The key points for a commercial biography:

■ Choose your subject carefully if you want the book to sell; someone genuinely famous, or genuinely interesting, or both.

■ Decide whose wishes need to be taken into account and consult them early on. You can't libel the dead, but you can certainly annoy their friends and relations. However, you will need to recognise that you are unlikely to be able to please everyone.

■ Decide what the central theme of the book will be and how you're going to present your subject – forgotten hero? Flawed genius? Tragic victim of history? All three? This will influence your choice of a title.

■ Make sure your book will be a *story*, with a beginning, a climax, cliffhangers and a conclusion. Remember that every book has to be a page-turner, unless it's a dictionary or the A-Z of London.

■ Explore your subject's world, starting with the places where he or she lived. If he liked collecting butterflies, find out what that involved at the time when he was doing it. If she was a diabetic, find out what it's like to live with diabetes.

■ Beware of taking a cradle-to-grave, no-stone-unturned approach unless your subject is of such importance to the world that *anything* new is of interest. And even then, focus and prioritise.

■ Start by consulting any previous biographical material, then move on to newspaper archives, official records, published works and the like.

■ Keep digging until you are sure you have the full story, at least in outline. Otherwise there is a danger that when the book comes out, people will ask how on earth you failed to mention your subject's time as a scout leader, or friendship with a famous actor.

■ Check your facts carefully, but don't be tempted to give anyone the right to approve your text unless it's a condition of writing the book.

CHAPTER 5

How not to write fiction

'As a writer you have only one job: to make the reader turn the page' – Sandra Newman & Howard Mittelmark, How Not To Write A Novel

It's easy to write a novel; all you need is time and something to type with. Unfortunately writing a good one, one that's worth reading, is difficult – very difficult.

What do I mean by a good novel? Here are the key elements.

Your **central character** or 'protagonist' must be someone the reader will identify with and care about, an original, credible and interesting blend of qualities and flaws. You might write about an unusual character in a relatively conventional situation (Lizzie Bennet in *Pride and Prejudice*), or you might place an ordinary person in an extraordinary situation (the dressing-gown-wearing, tea-drinking Arthur Dent in Douglas Adams' *The Hitchhiker's Guide to the Galaxy*). An ordinary person in an ordinary situation is not a promising start – unless of course one or the other turns out not to be ordinary after all. Placing an extraordinary person in an extraordinary situation is usually one extraordinary too many. There'll be nothing for the reader to identify with, nothing to make the remarkable bits seem remarkable.

The story must have an **objective** – getting the girl, finding the treasure, finding your true self, escaping from poverty, defeating the evil empire. This will give the narrative a vital sense of **direction**. The reader may not know how the objective is going to be achieved, but she should have the sense of being carried on an irresistible journey towards a satisfying conclusion. You'll have some idea what this might be from the opening chapter, though you may not know which girl is going to get the guy, or who will find the treasure, or how the hero will cast off his shackles, or how the monster will be overcome.

There will be a strong sense of **conflict** or adversity, of a major obstacle standing in the protagonist's way. A story without a proper challenge to be overcome (the bigger the better), is not a story at all – a principle adhered to from the nursery onward (the giant in *Jack and the Beanstalk*, the Ugly Sisters in *Cinderella*). Many novels by first-timers lack a decent obstacle; the talented girl who gets to the top of the fashion industry after overcoming nothing more irksome than a slightly sceptical boyfriend, or the tale of village life in which everything goes just fine, apart from some wet weather and a disagreement over the organ fund.

The obstacle may well be closely bound up with one of the

characters – a **villain**, who (if your story is any good) will not look like a villain, at least not at first (see below).

The protagonist will almost certainly undergo some sort of **journey,** metaphorical or actual (very likely both), through some kind of adversity to ultimate triumph or redemption.

How **happy** your story should be is entirely up to you; some people like happy endings, others despise them. Few people want to read a story in which everybody dies and the villain gets away with it, and not many readers like books in which no one dies and everyone lives happily ever after, except perhaps the nasty person who tried to murder the poor heroine, who jolly well goes to jail. But anywhere in between is fine.

Your protagonist may have a **sidekick**, a trusted ally whose loyalty is never doubted and whose bravery and comradeship will help him to reach his goal. Along the way your hero, with or without sidekick, will get **outside help**; perhaps from one particular person (a fairy godmother figure), perhaps a whole bunch of people (a tribe who share his enemy). Fairy godmothers don't have to have magical powers (they must not, of course, outside fairytales) – they just have to be in a position to give life-changing help at a crucial moment. The story will be more interesting if the fairy godmother is not the obvious person, like an ally or close friend. It might be a bullying teacher who turns out to have faith in her pupil, or a wealthy gentleman responding to an act of kindness (*The Railway Children*). A fairy godmother should not be invented only when she (or he) is needed – much better if she's introduced early on, with only a subtle hint of the magic wand she will wield later.

The **plot** – the bones of the story, the relationships between key events – must work, without loose ends or nonsensical developments, and lead to a satisfying conclusion which is neither predictable nor absurd. A well-crafted novel keeps two or three threads hanging in the air to tantalise the reader, then knits them together at the end in a way which is believable, yet unforeseen. This is a very difficult skill.

It must be **surprising**, and preferably shocking, without being implausible. I know I'm in for a yawn when I see that all the characters are called Peter Jones, Jane Andrews, Mary Jackson or David Carter, and that they live in conventional houses in a conventional village and do conventional things with conventional friends. The dialogue too is conventional; none of them ever say anything shocking, ridiculous, indiscreet or out of turn. I know by page 2 that there will be no twist in the tale and everything will end happily. Stories like this often appear to enact the author's own idea of what life ought to be like; I remember one (we didn't publish it) which was written by a woman who had left England many years before for a life in Canada. It was clear that she was writing the book to take herself on a trip down Memory Lane, and to immerse herself in an idealised England that had never existed. That's fine, as long as you realise that very few people will want to read such a book.

That twist in the tale is important, because predictable stories are plain boring. Many new writers think too small; the most shocking crime is the theft of a necklace, the biggest surprise is the news that the piano teacher has no qualifications. It's obvious from the first chapter that the town clerk is up to no good, and by chapter 3 we're getting broad hints that the spirited heroine and the nice new choirmaster will end up getting together.

How do you stop yourself from writing a predictable story? My suggestion is that you very gently lead the reader down a

blind alley or two. Say it's a murder story set in a quiet English village, and the murderer is going to turn out to be Martin Mullion, the local estate agent. Don't make Mr Mullion shifty or unpleasant; present him as genial, charming, virtuous. Have him make a generous donation to the organ fund, or rescue the heroine's cat. It will have more impact when his true nature is revealed later in the book. But while you're making Mr Mullion a picture of innocence, plant a little **clue**. Mention in passing (hidden innocuously among other mundane details about his house), that his cellar door has a new lock, or there's a pile of letters from the bank on his desk. Much later in the book we'll find out what he's keeping in the cellar that needed a secure lock, or discover that despite appearances he is in financial trouble, and it was he who killed Mrs Priestley, so that he could take a cut on the sale of her house.

Be careful, however, not to send the reader off on a wild goose chase by making too much of a detail which will play no further part in the story (a locked cellar which is never mentioned again).

If romance is part of your story, make sure there's an element of **competition**. No point in putting just one eligible young woman in your hero's life, because in doing so you're all but giving away the ending. Make sure there is at least one other plausible candidate for his affections. Again, you can lead the reader up the garden path. Set him up with Alice Amberley and create a reason why Betty Butterworth won't do, but then remove that reason later – perhaps Betty is married, but later we learn that her husband never came back from the war, or she's planning to go into a nunnery, but hasn't actually signed on the dotted line yet.

The most powerful tool of all in making the all-important

reader turn that all-important page is **suspense**. Suspense is created by setting up a situation in which the outcome is critical (to the protagonist, and therefore to us) but at the same time is highly uncertain, and it is invariably linked to some kind of danger. How will Rod escape from the well now that Farmer Wheatley has innocently sealed it up? Will the children get the message that the fairy cakes have been poisoned before they eat them? How far will Celia's date with Dr Potzinger get before she spots the clues that he is the rapist?

Having created suspense by posing such a question, for goodness' sake don't let your readers off the hook on the next page. You need to keep us (and Rod) hanging for a while. You can safely leave him in the well for a chapter or two while you describe what happened at the flower show. Don't worry, the reader won't forget about the poor chap, not if you've done a half-decent job of telling the story.

On a similar note, beware of what Newman and Mittelmark (*How Not to Write a Novel,* which, by the way, is essential reading for all would-be novelists) aptly call 'the benign tumour' – the problem which is safely turned into a non-event before it can make any difference to the story. If your protagonist is threatened with bankruptcy on page 73 and a rich uncle bails him out on page 75, you might as well not have bothered – unless, of course, he takes an overdose on page 74.

So suspense, and all the other factors we've talked about, must work together to make the reader want to turn the page, and make her want to keep on doing so until she gets to the end.

Of these, the three key factors, the ones your novel cannot do without, are the **protagonist**, the **objective** and the **challenge**. The whole story will be founded on these, so they must all be present and properly thought out. And they must match; they must all be right for each other.

Now you see why writing a novel with any chance of commercial success is so damn difficult, and why yours is not likely to work if you just start at the beginning, let the story develop as it will and finish when you've had enough. Successful novelists may write when the mood takes them and when ideas, words and names flood into their heads, but they also plan meticulously, then review and revise many times.

Study the competition

'Writing comes from reading, and reading is the finest teacher of how to write.' – Annie Proulx

I've already made the point that those who have been reading from the nursery make the best writers, and this is particularly true with fiction. Yet I get the impression from some of the novels sent to Mereo that the author has not read much work by other authors. This is like trying to bake a cake when you've never eaten one. As a result they make mistakes which a dedicated novel-reader would never make, such as messing up the use of voice (see Chapter 5) or making a pig's ear of their direct speech. They also tend to come up with ideas that have been used before ('I'm sending you my exciting new novel, which is about a white lawyer who is ostracised for defending a black criminal.'). The best preparation for writing in any genre is to read as much of that sort of book as you can, choosing the best, most successful authors, then try to come up with a story no one has told before. I told you becoming a novelist was not an overnight business.

In particular, you should read new titles that have very recently been published, because that will tell you what publishers are looking for now, which may be quite different from the stuff they were looking for ten years ago. New books by new authors are even more revealing, because each one of those represents a leap of faith by a publisher who has seen reason to invest tens of thousands in an unknown.

Avoiding the improbable

You can suspend disbelief big time in the basic idea for your story (a world in which lying has not been invented, a country where bears can talk, a bereaved wife whose love brings her husband back from the dead) but the details, whether it's fantasy or kitchen-sink, must be **believable**. People do not make long speeches after being riddled with bullets, security staff do not let casual visitors into factories in the middle of the night and middle-aged Sunday school teachers do not develop the ability to disarm three gunmen just because they are feeling cross.

Unlikely things may (and should) happen in novels, but don't write scenes which are patently absurd. One writer described how his hero, having broken into the villains' stronghold without being detected, stumbled upon them chatting around the dinner table and was able to watch from the shadows unnoticed as they explained every detail of their dastardly plans to each other, conveniently addressing one another by their full names. Enid Blyton could get away with it; you can't.

Try to maintain a decent **pace,** but also to vary it, like the composer of a symphony. Important episodes need to be painted in precise detail, while routine matters – things the reader can fill in themselves, such as the business of travelling from one place to another (assuming the journey isn't important to your story) – should be dealt with in shorthand. Try not to let your characters sit around talking for too long. Things need to happen, particularly in an adventure story, or a crime novel or thriller.

The pointless excursion

Don't write about anything that doesn't have a **job to do** in your novel. Introduce a cat if it is going to be used to demonstrate a character's cruelty or soft-heartedness, not because you like cats. Describe a storm if it will cause a shipwreck, not because you enjoy writing about weather. Don't take your protagonist on a day trip to a stately home unless you're doing it so that she can catch Mr Prendergast holding Mrs Montgomery's hand in the tea rooms. Don't prattle about sporting events, shopping trips or wayward household appliances, or anything else, unless this will help the reader understand your characters or your story better.

And on that note, don't introduce spare characters just for fun. If they don't form part of the plot, or at least part of the setting, they are nothing more than distractions. By all means bring in a comedy vicar to give us a few laughs in chapter 5 if in chapter 11 he turns out to be the one who deliberately mixed up the babies.

A word about length

How long should your novel be? (We're talking words, not pages – telling a publisher your book is '100 pages' is like a farmer measuring his land in fields – depending on font, size and spacing, an A4 page can accommodate anything from 200 words to 1000 or so.) Use Word Count to give you the figure – one reason why it's best to write your book on a single computer file, see Chapter 16. A typical novel is around 60,000-120,000 words. Anything less than about 40,000 words is really a novella (a baby novel), and novellas are not popular with publishers, or with readers, who may feel short-changed, although eBooks, being that much cheaper, have tended to make short books more acceptable. If you go much over 120,000, your novel had better be good. Apart from anything else, if you're self-publishing many of your costs will go up almost pro rata.

Beware of padding

Don't make the mistake of writing more just for the sake of making your book long enough. I have seen manuscripts where it was clear that the author had thought something like: 'Books are really long, aren't they? I'm going to need lots of words. I'd better describe every scene as thoroughly as possible.' The result is padding – an 11-page description of two people having a cup of coffee, or the lead character's feelings at being dumped by her boyfriend described over and over again in slightly different ways. If your MS needs padding to get to novel length, you're going to have to develop the story.

A single sentence can be guilty of padding. I see this sort of thing all the time:

Carol could not see the funny side, nor did she understand why her friends were laughing.

That's just the same thing said twice.

Mr Ravenscroft always had a warm welcome, a friendly smile and a kind word for each new apprentice.

These three ideas go hand in hand, so you need only mention one of them to denote Mr Ravenscroft's friendliness.

Period and setting

Choose a place and a period you are comfortable with, and can write well about. You can write a scene set in New York without ever having been there (with a little research), but to set a whole novel there would be foolhardy. And if your knowledge of the reign of King George III is confined to reading *Pride and Prejudice*, you'd best steer clear, or do plenty of homework. If you choose a setting you happen to know well but which will not be familiar to most readers – the Isle of Man, Nova Scotia or Vanuatu – you're giving yourself a head start, because you'll be able to create a really strong background, and even better, the setting itself will give you ideas for characters and storylines.

When you're setting part of your story in a country that's unfamiliar to you, be wary of using terms which are peculiar to the UK. I've seen an English writer refer to a French doctor as a GP, and another describing an American getting his P45.

By all means use the names of real people, brands and organisations to add authenticity to your story. Ian Fleming was perhaps the first novelist to feature real brands in a big way, in the James Bond novels – I can remember as a teenager being deeply impressed by his references to Martini, Dom Pérignon,

Kina Lillet, Rolex, Red Stripe beer, and of course the Bentleys, Aston Martins and Berettas. There appears to be a myth among many amateur writers (as mentioned in chapter 4) that there is something wrong with naming real products and organisations in a book – not so, as long as you don't libel them (see page 49).

Point of view

'It's harder to write in the third person, but the advantage is you move around better.' – Ernest Hemingway

Before you start writing, you'll need to choose your point of view. You have two options; first person (I) or third person (he/she). The first person works fine when you want all the focus to be on your protagonist's experiences, thoughts and feelings, but it is limited in that everything in your story has to be told from his/her point of view; you can't step outside your hero's head to describe how someone else is feeling, or tell the reader what happened when he or she was not around to see it. Say your protagonist has a row with her boyfriend and storms out of his house, and as her car roars off down the road her younger sister emerges naked from his bathroom. You can't tell the reader any of this until your heroine finds out about it, hours, days or years later. If she never finds out what her sister's been up to, you can't tell the reader at all. So if you want to focus all your attention on the main character and are happy to let the story unfold through her eyes, an 'I' book is fine. Otherwise, stick to the third person.

It's important to appreciate, however, that when writing in the third person you still have be careful about your point of view:

Olivia let out a silent gasp of relief. So this ragged young man was no mugger or rapist. He was merely an estate worker who had been sent by her uncle to warn her about the gypsies.

'But how did you find me?' she asked him.

A frown spread across Norman Oakshott's face. What was he to say? He did not dare to tell her that he had been watching her from the shadows for the best part of twenty minutes.

I'd say this (invented) passage reads uncomfortably, because the reader has unceremoniously been wrenched out of Olivia's head and thrust inside Norman's instead. The writer has used internal monologue (see below) to describe what Olivia is thinking, and then to tell us what Norman is thinking. You shouldn't do that to readers. If the writer wanted to tell us that Norman was hiding something, she should have done it by describing his furtive behaviour as seen by Olivia, or through dialogue. The rule, even in the third person, is to keep to the protagonist's point of view. You have to tell the story as if you were sitting on your lead character's shoulder, with a hotline to her thoughts as she observes the story unfold. You might pull your viewpoint back for a moment to describe the scene in general ('evening was now drawing on and lights were beginning to twinkle further down the valley'), but you can't casually jump from one person's shoulder to another for a couple of sentences, as in the example above; you'll dislocate the narrative and leave the reader reeling.

Even one word can trip you up:

He smiled, certain I would be pleased at the news.

That word 'certain' again takes you into forbidden territory, because your protagonist can't know the man's thoughts. This is an easy fix, though – just insert a word like 'obviously' before 'certain'.

So you shouldn't change heads within a scene, but you can do it if you start a new one. To describe how the world is looking from Norman Oakshott's point of view, the writer could start a new chapter or section: 'Norman was grinning to himself as he plodded back to his hut in the clearing. So this was the Parbold girl they were all talking about…' Then you can return to Olivia in the next scene. The freedom to do this is one of the key advantages of writing in the third person.

You can if you wish use something which has been called the 'omniscient third person'. This is when the writer takes a stance in which he knows more, perhaps far more, than the protagonist does about the world in which the story is unfolding, and imparts information to the reader to fill in the background and move the tale along, rather like the chorus in Shakespeare's *Henry V*.

And as he drove on, the rainclouds dragged down the sky after him, for though he did not know it, Rob McKenna was a Rain God. All he knew was that his working days were miserable and he had had a succession of lousy holidays. All the clouds knew was that they loved him and wanted to be near him, to cherish him, and to water him. – Douglas Adams, So Long and Thanks For All the Fish

The level of omniscience is up to you, as long as you're consistent through the book. You can tell us anything and everything that the characters don't know, which can be entertaining in a light-hearted novel ('Poor Rodney. It was such a shame that no one had told him that Sasha's real name was Sean, and by day she worked on a building site') or you can just give us glimpses.

Don't make the mistake of adding just a little omniscience – of slipping comments about what's going on into a book which so far has been written without an observer. That's like a character in a conventional TV drama suddenly turning to say something to the camera. A statement in the narrative like 'Poor Rodney never worked there again' or 'It must be said that he was wrong' will look very odd, as if the author has suddenly decided to relate his tale like a fireside storyteller.

In the third person as in the first, you can't hit us with stuff that is not, and cannot be, known to your character:

Stefan opened the door to find himself in a large, expensively-furnished hall which was used by the President for entertaining overseas visitors.

Stefan couldn't know this, though he might be able to deduce it from what he saw. You'd have to write something like this:

Stefan opened the door to find himself in a large hall. Judging by the expensive furniture and the lavishly-stocked bar, this was the room the President used for entertaining overseas visitors.

The silent observer

At the opposite extreme from the omniscient third person is what you might call the ignorant third person. This is where no information is given about what people are thinking and feeling, even the protagonist, through their heads or anyone else's; you have to work everything out by following the action and listening to the dialogue, almost as if you were reading the script of a play or film. John Steinbeck's much-studied *Of Mice And Men* is an example of this rare approach.

Some amateur 'I' writers, usually autobiographers, describe themselves as if observed from the outside, just like their other characters. This can read very oddly: 'A smile crept across my face', 'I watched with an air of hidden amusement' (both real examples). Remember that when you're writing an 'I' book, all your observations have to come from inside your own head.

Internal monologue

The question of point of view is closely linked to **internal monologue**. You may not be familiar with that term, but you will have seen it many times in story-telling. It's the formal name for what happens when you continue the narrative by describing what your protagonist is thinking or feeling:

The third possibility was to try to sort out in his mind just what he had become involved in. Where did Macbride and Annie fit into it? Where was Annie now? Would O'Donnell carry out his threat of informing the police if he decided to give the whole thing the heave-ho? As yet he had no answers to any of these questions, but he felt the risk of calling O'Donnell's bluff was too high. He would just have to go along with things, at least for a while. – Stay Lucky, *Peter Minto (Mereo, 2015)*

The discovery of internal monologue comes as a revelation to those authors who thought the only way to tell the reader what their characters were thinking was to make them talk to themselves, complete with quote marks. If you've already written a book on this understanding, you (or your editor) is going to have a lot of work to do to put it right.

Getting started

You must plan out your novel thoroughly before you do any writing.

No! If the urge to write is upon you, hit the keyboard while the creative juices are flowing. You can always sort it out later.

Which is it to be? A bit of both, it seems to me. A lot depends on the seed from which your story is to grow. It might be a particular person, a situation, a scene, that appeals to you; even a single phrase. I once built an idea for a novel around a controlling, obsessive husband, simply because it occurred to me that I could describe him very neatly as 'editing the vegetables' for a meal (he was a newspaper editor). It didn't get very far because I didn't want to write about someone with OCD. Or indeed about an editor.

Some authors can set off on a fictional journey with an idea of where they are going and make the whole story stay on course and make sense. Most can't, so I suggest you do as much planning as you reasonably can.

Decide what your story is about, start developing a plot and work out what characters you are going to need. Have an ending in mind, even though you may decide to change it later. Every part of the book should be written to contribute to the book as a whole.

Structure

By far the simplest way of writing a novel is to start at the beginning (chronologically, I mean) and end at the end. Plenty of novelists have broken this rule, and some have done so successfully, such as Martin Amis, who wrote *Time's Arrow* backwards. But if you're new to the game, I suggest you stick to chronological order.

This doesn't rule out using such devices as flashbacks, in which the protagonist remembers an earlier event which is important to the story, or the 'flashforward', in which he or she takes us to a time and place which belongs much later in the novel, in order to arouse our curiosity and prepare us for what will be unveiled in the pages to come. The flashforward is a powerful technique for hooking the reader by engaging them in the plot up front. You could, for example, use a single-page flashforward at the start of a thriller to describe how Matilda McCafferty is found dead on a tropical beach. Now it's on with Chapter One, and we meet Matilda larger than life and living in Surbiton, with no indication that any harm is going to come to her, or that she is going to be travelling any further than Thames Ditton. What is going on? That little scene immediately whets the reader's appetite and gives her something to think about. The flashforward is a way of engaging the reader early on, and of raising questions in her mind which are more specific and intriguing than 'I wonder if this novel's going to be any good'.

The prologue in fiction

That little scene about Matilda McCafferty is in fact a form of prologue. Properly used, a prologue can be a cunning device to get a story under way and draw the reader in early, just as it can in non-fiction. The next author has used a short one to pretend to the reader that he is about to tell a true story (this one's about dragons). The level of detail surrounding the discovery of the box is the author's way of telling us its contents are going to be very, very interesting, so you'd better pay attention:

Some years ago we bought an old, neglected longhouse in Netherbury, Dorset. At the rear stood a range of old stables and animal feed rooms. One stable was piled to the eaves with logs cut from old trees, so many that it took us ten winters to burn them all on the fire.

One spring as the pile was coming down somewhat, I set to work to sort the logs out, restacking them and clearing the floor. Concealed behind them I found a large and dusty tin box, sealed with what looked like candle wax. When I managed to open it I found it contained a pile of yellowed paper.

I took it into the house to study it, to find that in my hands I was holding the manuscript of a book; in fact, two books. I was stunned by what I read.

This is the first volume. I wonder what you will make of it.

Steve Davis, The Merlin Legacy *(Mereo, 2012)*

Evelyn Waugh began *Brideshead Revisited*, arguably his finest novel, with a 16-page prologue in which the protagonist, Charles Ryder, who is serving as a junior army officer in World War II, finds himself and his men billeted at a stately home which has been commandeered by the army; it is none other than Brideshead Castle, the place where the momentous events of Ryder's youth took place twenty years before. The whole of the rest of the book is set in that earlier time. The prologue ends with Ryder's platoon commander describing the place where they have just arrived. As he talks, Ryder realises with a shock that he knows it only too well:

'There's a frightful great fountain, too, in front of the steps, all rocks and sort of carved animals. You never saw such a thing.'

'Yes Hooper, I did. I've been here before.'

The words seemed to ring back to me enriched from the vaults of my dungeon.

'Oh well, you know all about it. I'll go and get cleaned up.'

I had been there before; I knew all about it.

Chapter One begins:

I had been there before; first with Sebastian more than twenty years ago on a cloudless day in June, when the ditches were creamy with meadowsweet and the air heavy with all the scents of summer; it was a day of peculiar splendour, and though I had been there so often, in so many moods, it was to that first visit that my heart returned on this, my latest.

Brideshead Revisited, *1945*

I hope you agree that it is difficult not to read on after a beginning like that.

The beginning

'There is something delicious about writing the first words of a story. You never quite know where they'll take you.' — *Beatrix Potter*

Prologue or not, the first few paragraphs of a novel are very important, not least because a lot of people (I hope) will read yours in the bookstore or on the Amazon website and decide there and then whether or not to bother with your book. So will a publisher. The first page or so of your novel needs to have enough impact to make you want to read on. It also has to start the story off, which many amateur novels fail to do (we get pages and pages of scene-setting and character introduction before we are allowed to find out what is going to happen).

So let's see some examples.

Here the author establishes the authority of his story at once by presenting it as if it were a factual account:

Squire Trelawney, Dr Livesey, and the rest of these gentlemen having asked me to write down the whole particulars about Treasure Island, from the beginning to the end, keeping nothing back but the bearings of the island, and that only because there is still treasure not yet lifted, I take up my pen in the year of grace 17— and go back to the time when my father kept the 'Admiral Benbow' inn and the brown old seaman with the sabre cut first took up his lodging under our roof.
- Robert Louis Stevenson, Treasure Island *(1883)*

This famous opening tells us what the rest of the book is going to be about in just 23 words:

It is a truth universally acknowledged that a single man in possession of a good fortune, must be in want of a wife.
– Jane Austen, Pride and Prejudice (1813)

Here's a master novelist plunging his reader into the story before he has a chance to resist:

Hale knew, before he had been in Brighton three hours, that they meant to murder him. – Brighton Rock, *Graham Greene (1938)*

And this is even shorter:

Ten days after the war ended my sister Laura drove a car off a bridge. – The Blind Assassin, *Margaret Atwood (McClelland and Stewart, 2000)*

The opening sentence of this best-seller is so startling that only the dullest of readers could resist the temptation to read on:

My name was Salmon, like the fish; first name, Susie. I was fourteen when I was murdered on December 6, 1973. – The Lovely Bones, *Alice Sebold (Picador, 2002)*

Novels don't have to start with a shock like that, and indeed most don't, but you do need to capture your reader well before she has got to the foot of the first page.

Time travel

If you've decided to write a novel which is set in an age other than your own, you have given yourself an extra challenge, particularly when it comes to direct speech. You don't have to be an expert on Victorian London to write a story based on Jack the Ripper, nor do you have to be a student of vernacular

Victorian English, but you do have to be able to write in a way which won't have your reader doubled up with laughter at every other sentence.

It can be remarkably difficult to sound convincing when adopting a voice that is far removed from your own in time or place. A story I once worked on was based on the experiences of a homeless teenage girl in early Victorian London who talked freely of 'body language' and her 'family unit' and of 'liaising' with the authorities. I don't think ten-year-olds use those words now, and I'm damn sure they didn't in 1840. One historical romance had a Regency buck talk about a 'worst-case scenario'. Then we had the Victorian landlord who offered guests a 'full English breakfast', while a children's author created a goblin home which had a lounge and a patio.

Some authors can't resist the temptation to have their characters make uncannily prescient statements about the future:

'Today most people never leave the parish where they were born, but that will all change.'

'You mark my words, they motor things will be tekkin' over from horses and carts by about 1925.'

'I shouldn't be surprised if thirty years from now the whole of Barton Lane is knocked down to make way for a new hospital for cancer patients.'

It's a temptation which should be resisted.

Creating characters

'If you're silent for a long time, people just arrive in your mind.'
– Alice Walker

Don't let the word 'character' fool you – your characters have to be *people,* and as real as you can make them. Base them on real people or make them up, or a bit of both, as you wish. Characters need to be rooted in the familiar (a retired bank manager, a penniless housewife), but be defined by something unexpected; a retired bank manager who never knew his parents, a penniless housewife who makes a living after dark in a strip club. The physical attributes of your characters are less important than *who* they are; their natures and personalities.

Nevertheless you should get the hard facts out of the way as soon as you introduce them, or you will confuse readers. If you bring a 'young girl' into the room, your reader might imagine you're talking about an eight-year-old. If you leave it for half a page before you mention that actually this young girl is seventeen, he'll have to repaint the picture in his mind's eye. If two pages further on you remember to tell us that she is severely overweight, he'll have to tear up that mental picture too.

You will need to start painting a picture of your lead character at the beginning, but don't make the mistake of doing it by devoting pages to describing his routine – climbing out of bed, shaving, dressing, making a phone call, travelling to work, greeting his colleagues etc, because you are giving the reader every reason to dismiss him as boring. Much better to start with something different happening to him; an odd letter in the post, a stranger at the door, being sent on an unusual assignment, getting the sack.

Work out what characters your story is going to need, and don't add extra ones without good reason. Many amateur novels are full of undifferentiated people – all the protagonist's workmates are the same blokeish, matey stereotype, or all her girlfriends whoop and banter with the same voice.

Filling in the background

'All those words (horrifying, wonderful, hideous, exquisite) are only like saying to your readers, "Please will you do my job for me."' – C S Lewis

There is no point in telling us that the scenery was 'amazing', the landscape 'awesome', the food 'unbelievable' or the weather 'terrible'. These are words for inarticulate or lazy writers (though you could put them in a character's mouth, to show that he/she doesn't have much of interest to say). Show the reader, in words, just what was amazing, awesome, unbelievable or terrible about it.

Your places should be characters just like your people, in fiction as in factual books. Never short-change the reader with picture-postcard adjectives. It makes life easier if you avoid writing about places you don't know, but if you have to, do some research. The internet allows you to cheat; Google Earth and its Streetview option will put you almost anywhere on the planet, as mentioned earlier.

The joy of names

As mentioned in the section about vital novel ingredients, new authors often seem to neglect the pleasure of choosing good names for their characters, and lazily call everyone John, Jane or Mr Jones. In truth, the names of fictional characters deserve considerable thought. To quote the novelist and professor of literature David Lodge: 'In a novel names are never neutral. They always signify, if it is only ordinariness'.

In real life names often don't fit the people they belong to – in a novel, they can and should, however subtly, either through the meaning of the name or its associations. In Margaret Mitchell's *Gone With The Wind*, Scarlett O'Hara was a wonderful name for a vivacious, beautiful, fiery woman. More subtly, Mitchell chose Ashley Wilkes' first name for its connotation of pallor, symbolising the death of the Confederate cause. You might pick a name like Mr Driswell, Mrs Fussell, Christian, Virginia or Randy for its obvious overtones, or choose names to reflect the class, age group or background you are describing, as long as you avoid the boringly obvious – not all elderly aunts are called Agatha or Gertrude. You could go deeper and check the original meanings of names for another layer of significance – Philip means horse-lover, for example, and Stark is the German for strong. There's a useful website for checking the meanings of first names at www.behindthename.com.

Avoid the obvious – Brett, Darcy, Scarlett, Kate, Rebecca and so on for the names of romantic heroes and heroines have all been done to death. Don't give a villain an unusual name that might actually belong to someone, because if there is just one Sebastian J Skrank out there he might sue. Beware of descending to farce (Mr Wollygolly, Mrs Splutter) unless of course you are writing a farce, or a children's book.

A good tip is to notice and collect names from the real world and use them as needed in your writings. The *Hitchhiker's Guide to the Galaxy* series author Douglas Adams named a swashbuckling character Hotblack Desiato, after a London estate agency (the firm is still going strong, unlike, sadly, Adams).

A character who hasn't been given a name isn't just a source of confusion for the reader – he's a missed opportunity. Never pass up the chance to give someone a satisfying name. Talking about the doings of 'Lord Radcliffe's housekeeper' or 'Wayne's girlfriend' without endowing them with a name, and the right name, is like selling chocolates by numbers, yet we editors see this often. Names are fun, and help enormously with your characterisation. They also act as a sort of shorthand. We'll see Lord Radcliffe's housekeeper one way if she's called Miss Privet and quite another if she is Mrs Understone, and calling Wayne's girlfriend Catastrophia will tell us more than a paragraph of description of her wild eyes and drug-induced hairstyle. Incidentally, never describe a character by his or her similarity to a real person, because in the reader's mind, they will instantly become that person.

Please don't change your protagonist's name halfway through. I've seen this done, and it's disastrous. If your lead character is a social climber who changes her name from Clarrie to Camilla after getting lucky with a baronet, she is still Clarrie to the reader, and she always will be, even if the other characters now call her Camilla. This rule cannot be broken.

What about names of places? They need to be interesting too, and there is great scope for playing on words and double meanings, particularly in light-hearted books – Endsmeet, Little Smattering. Again, it's a good plan to notice and note down satisfying real place names you see on your travels – my collection contains Ashbrittle, Dreghorn, Scurlage and Yarpole.

Weaving the narrative

So let's say you have your protagonist, a couple of supporting characters (you will doubtless introduce others as you go) and a basic direction for the book. You've defined the big challenge your protagonist will face, and you have a pretty good idea what's going to get in her way. You have a period, and a setting. You've decided on a voice, a setting and a time.

How do you start putting the narrative together?

I suspect that every novelist would give a different answer to this. I'm pretty sure that if you feel the urge to write, you should just write. You never quite know what's going to happen until you put pen to paper. Although you may have imagined at first that your heroine should occupy a dowdy bedsit, you may surprise yourself by realising at the end of the first chapter that she really ought to be in a smart modern flat. Your characters and settings will develop lives of their own, or should do, if you're any good at this game.

Yet you need to come back to your plan. If for the sake of the story your protagonist is going to spend a large part of the book working as an agricultural labourer, don't give him a rich father in Chapter One. If she's going to dash off and sail round the world, it's no good endowing her with a withered arm, or two small children – unless, of course, that's exactly the point of the story. Keep – in outline at least – to the script.

Here those budding authors who write as if they were

putting together a film script turn out to be onto something – telling your story is indeed going to involve presenting a series of scenes, though they will be described through the eyes and thoughts of your protagonist, not literally through a camera lens. The more vividly and convincingly each of them is portrayed, the better your novel is likely to be. At the same time you have to carry the story forward, developing the plot and the characters as you go.

Each scene will have at least one job to do. Let's say your heroine is a frustrated shopgirl called Wazira who longs to be a professional dancer, and the obstacles you're going to put in her way are poverty, unsympathetic parents and total ignorance of the realities of show business. Set up your first scene to reveal these things, by showing her eating with her family. We'll learn from their conversation what a struggle it is for her parents to put food on the table, and how scornful her mother and father are of her ambitions (or perhaps one's in favour, one against). If just her father is against her, what's her mother going to do – row with her husband about it, or find a way of helping her daughter on the quiet? If both of them are against her plan, who will come out of the woodwork to help her – who will be her fairy godmother? Perhaps she has a decrepit grandfather, ignored by most of the family, who happens to have a secret stash of money which he offers to put towards Wazira's training. Or perhaps eccentric Mrs Satsuma next door turns out to have once been a famous dance teacher…

I'm beginning to enjoy this, and I only made it up as an example. We may not learn all the above in the first chapter (certainly not about Mrs Satsuma being a dance teacher, it's much too soon for that), but we'll understand Wazira's fix and the world she lives in, and how difficult it's going to be for her to get where she wants to go. Poor Wazira! Whatever will she do? Now read on to find out…

Description

'Don't tell me the moon is shining; show me the glint of light on broken glass.' — Anton Chekhov

It's important to put the reader into the settings where the action in your story takes place, and the more important the scene, the more important the description. You often sense when you're reading a well-written book (fact or fiction) that something big is going to happen in a particular place, just from the loving detail with which the author opens the scene. And that's the key – interesting, original detail.

Try to weave a personal viewpoint into descriptive passages to make them come to life. When you describe a building, for example, don't run through its features like an estate agent's brochure – tell us how your character pushed the door open and what he found as he explored:

The hall was high and dark, with bare walls decorated only by the ghostly outlines of long-removed paintings. At the far side was an ostentatious inglenook fireplace, anguished and desolate. I looked around. Several rooms led off the hallway, all identically depressing; I stepped into the first one to see an empty grate and a large and ugly mantelpiece. The bare treads of the spiral staircase were covered in a litter of refuse, old letters, papers and countless generations of beetle bodies, a few live and scurrying ones still among them.

– Catacombs of the Damned, *P J Cadavori (Mereo, 2013)*

There's a knack to really good description. I can't tell you how to acquire it, but I'll show you how it can look:

From the window he could see part of Parnassus Road, wide and empty as an airport runway, lying stunned under the afternoon sun. Along the strip of shops a few cars were parked diagonally into the gutters liker tadpoles nosing up to a rock. A dog lay stretched out lifeless across the doorway of an empty shop. The awnings over the shops made jagged blocks of black shadow and the great radiance of the sun pressed down out of the sky.

- The Idea of Perfection, *Kate Grenville (Pan Macmillan, 1999)*

Note how the above author has made her description striking and original by using words you don't usually associate with one another – the road is stunned, the cars are like tadpoles, the sun presses. This is the exact opposite of cliché.

Many authors write with their eyes only, entirely forgetting the other senses. Adding sounds or smells to the description will help enormously, particularly in bringing critical passages to life. How are you going to make your hero realise that the mysterious man in the back of the car is the same one he grappled with in a dark alley on Tuesday night? Perhaps a distinctive smell will give him away, or perhaps he will start humming the same tune.

Before Steadman could finish, the man had brushed past him and was already opening the box. His footsteps were light and almost silent. He must be wearing trainers or crepe sole shoes; odd for a tradesman. Then there was a loud click. The electricity had gone off. The hair on the back of Steadman's neck prickled… – Blind Pursuit, *John Buchan (Mereo 2013)*

Be specific

'Experience is communicated by small details intimately observed.' – Ernest Hemingway

All too often, less accomplished writers describe scenes vaguely, with no attempt at detail. It's clear that the mental picture the description is based on must also have been vague and ill-thought-out.

One of the latest hits was playing on the radio and she started dancing around the kitchen.

Why not tell us what the song was, with a snatch of the lyrics, and describe how she was dancing?

She opened the door to find the police standing there.

What, all of them? Let's hear how many officers were there, whether male or female, and if one of them was carrying a clipboard, a lost kitten or a gun. And 'they' can't speak – it has to be one of them; the red-haired one, the tall one, the male one, the woman.

Clem stepped out into the street. It was cold and damp and there was melting snow and slush everywhere.

This could be any street in any city on Earth in any latitude above 60 degrees, on any winter's day. It's far too vague to be interesting. Try this:

Clem stepped out onto the slush-covered pavement, almost slipping on a soggy Kentucky Fried Chicken wrapper which had emerged from the melting ice like the garment of a long-frozen corpse. On the other side of Tallahassee Street he could see Mr Gonzales scraping snow from the roof of his grey Volvo estate with what looked like a broken tennis racket.

I think this effort of mine may be a little over the top, but don't you think it's more absorbing? This is because the scene described is far more detailed, far more specific. There's something for the reader to get his teeth into.

Cut out the fat

Many authors get carried away with their keyboards, churning out long passages which do not advance the story or tell us anything useful:

Roger nosed the Jaguar out on to the A603. The traffic was even worse than it had been yesterday, and it had been pretty bad then. Within another mile the traffic in all three lanes was slowly grinding to a halt while still creeping at a snail's pace in the inside lane, and he could see a long line of cars and lorries winding their way all the way up the hill and beyond. He could see that some of the drivers ahead had got out of the cars to see what was going on. 'Why the hell don't the fools put a warning up before the junction instead of after it' he thought to himself, then he could have come off the motorway and gone the back way through Ashbrittle, Bogborough and Clulow. Now he was going to be really late, probably at least 20 minutes. He had a good mind to write to his MP about it. This was the sort of thing that was dragging Britain into…

This is just inconsequential prattle. A traffic delay might indeed be used to make your character arrive at work late and angry, so that he makes a bad business decision which affects the course of the story, but you don't need all the humdrum detail – we get enough of that sort of thing in real life. A few lines would do the job:

As Roger nosed the Jaguar out on to the A603, his grin faded. He had missed a diversion sign and driven into the mother and father of traffic jams. By the time he had extricated himself from it, twenty precious minutes had passed and he knew there was no chance of making the meeting on time.

The climax

If your novel is going to come to a dramatic conclusion (I hope it is) you need to set it up; you have to fashion it from pre-existing ingredients, elements which you built into your story much earlier on. You can't just invent a way of getting everyone out of the fix they're in. If the pilot is going to save the plane and its passengers with his mastery of martial arts, the fact that he has that skill needs to be brought in much earlier in the story, as an innocent piece of background. If the heroine is going to decide at the last minute to spurn an offer of romance and ride off into the sunset alone, we need to have seen evidence much earlier on that this could be part of her nature, or some plausible reason for her to make this decision must have been built into the story, such as an early emotional experience which made her grow up unable to trust men.

The End

It can be as difficult to end a book satisfactorily as it is to begin it. Many a new writer complains that her last sentence reads as if the book is unfinished, and doesn't know what to do about it:

I asked Jane what would happen to Jim. 'Oh he'll be charged with kidnapping, there's no doubt about that, and given the prison sentence he deserves,' she said. I burst into tears at the thought of my brother being locked in a prison cell.

This reads as if there is more to come, but there wasn't. With the editor's help it could be rewritten more like this:

When he added that Jim had been charged with kidnapping and given a prison sentence I could not hold back the tears, thinking of what my brother had been through and fearful at the thought of him being locked away in a prison cell. And then I looked across at my daughter's innocent face and knew that finally, I had done something right.

Here is the last paragraph of one of my favourite books (it's not a novel, though these lines would do fine in a first-person one), in which the author remembers his beloved father:

I like to think that he found his lonely creek, and that he lies always by the sea-lavender-covered marshlands, where there is no sound but a distant sea and the curlews crying. He was a very kind man. – Hugh Falkus, The Stolen Years *(1965)*

That simple, short last sentence finishes the job beautifully. Or you can use a few lines of lyrical description as a closer:

As Max's slim form disappeared into the distance, Letitia wiped a stray tear away and looked out at the blustery Fenland landscape. The cawing of the rooks in the elms at the top of the hill reminded her that spring would soon be arriving. She turned to walk back to the Manse. Now, at last, she knew that she and Seth would never be apart again.

There are other ways of doing it. To avoid leaving the narrative looking as if there's a page missing off the end, you can try a number of devices. First, the jocular summing-up remark, and the cheerful return to mundanity:

'I'll say one thing, Doc. I don't think either of us is going to be visiting any more caves again for a very long time. Come on, let's go for a pint.'

'Don't worry my dear, I very much doubt if we will be hearing of Professor Calliper again. Now, where that's damned paper. I'm going to finish the crossword if it kills me.'

Incidentally, you really don't have to write the 'THE END' at the foot of the last chapter. It's going to be kind of obvious from the fact that there's no more text. You won't find it appearing in many adult novels these days.

The title

I've left this till last because with fiction, the title is often the last thing to emerge during the creative process (I never try to think up a title for someone else's book until I have worked on it). Titles are funny things. Sometimes they leap out at you instantly; in fact a good idea for a title may be the spark that sets the book off. In other cases it's a nightmare to find one that seems to work.

Your title needs to do certain things:

■ Make your book look interesting.

■ Make it look literate and accomplished, without being pretentious.

■ Reflect the *flavour* of the book; a violent action novel needs a violent, action-packed title and a funny one calls for a witty title, while a profound and clever literary novel needs something deep and subtle. You wouldn't want to call a novel about war 'The Green Teddy Bear' for the sake of symbolism, however much your mum might like it, and you wouldn't want to title a raunchy bodice-ripper 'Love Among the Lupins'. Probably.

■ Be short enough to stand out boldly on the cover, even at web page thumbnail size (I know there are exceptions to this, but it's still a good guideline).

■ Be original – preferably unique. Not just to avoid confusion on the net, but so that people will think, 'Gosh, that sounds interesting'.

Most authors struggle with titles and come up with ideas that just won't work. Did you know that one of the titles F Scott Fitzgerald originally proposed for *The Great Gatsby* was *Trimalchio in West Egg*? And Charles Dickens jotted down 14 title ideas for *Hard Times* before he made his decision.

Many of the great novels of history have very bland titles, but back then there was no internet, and we weren't publishing hundreds of thousands of novels a year. These days your title has to fight for your book.

Some tricks to get you thinking along the right lines:

■ Use the protagonist's name or job description – *Jane Eyre, Nicholas Nickleby, The Governess, The Horse Whisperer.*

■ Call the novel after the setting – *Athabasca, Uncle Tom's Cabin, The Old Curiosity Shop.*

■ Use an apposite line from great literature, particularly the Bible and Shakespeare – *The Grapes of Wrath, This Happy Breed, A Handful of Dust.* This approach is however a little outmoded these days.

■ Use the title to sum up the protagonist's situation – *The Last of the Mohicans.*

■ Find words to summarise the theme of the book – *Pride and Prejudice.*

■ Name the key elements in the story – *The Old Man and the Sea, The Lion, The Witch and The Wardrobe.*

■ Use a key phrase from the book – *Fahrenheit 451, High Fidelity.*

Here are some more titles that work well:

Blind Pursuit
Snappy, powerful, and a double meaning – a blind man is hunted by killers.

The Five Hundred Year War
Enigmatic and dramatic.

The Lines of Tamar
An intriguing hint of the occult, like *The Da Vinci Code.*

What about a pen name?

Some authors prefer to write under a made-up name, either because they don't want readers to know their true identity or because they feel their own name doesn't sound snappy enough for a novelist (Joseph Conrad's real name was Jozef Teodor Konrad Korzeniowski, John le Carré's is David Cornwell). Full-time authors may use more than one name, because they are writing in two different genres, for example. The one-time Poet Laureate Cecil Day-Lewis wrote thrillers as Nicolas Blake, and Kingsley Amis wrote a James Bond novel (post-Ian Fleming) as Robert Markham.

Names do make a big difference to the assumptions people make about you, as pop stars and film stars know. Distinctiveness is also important – who would remember an author called Dave Smith? (sorry Dave). So if your real name is Ethel Shufflebottom or Damien Drool you might want to change it – or trade on it. Your call.

A word about sequels

If you can write a novel that lends itself to a sequel or two, you might be on to a winner. A sequel gives you the chance to build up a following, and as new readers join your fan club, so sales of your earlier books will pick up.

Beware however of thinking you can write a big-picture novel and then follow it up with another great story involving the same characters. If you have made a decent job of your first book, your character has nowhere to go; their story is finished. Winding up Lizzie Bennet in *Pride and Prejudice* or Atticus Finch in *To Kill A Mockingbird* and expecting them to be interesting all over again is not going to work. Sequels may well make sense, however, when the first book does not tell a character's whole story; Thomas Hughes left himself plenty of room to write a sequel to *Tom Brown's Schooldays* (not that he ever did so).

Sequels are no problem of course if you are writing adventure, crime or sci-fi novels. Once you've invented a decent hero you can put him or her through the mill as many times as you like; think of Allan Quartermain in *King Solomon's Mines*, Patricia Cornwell's Kay Scarpetta, Sherlock Holmes or James Bond.

Short stories

'A short story must have a single mood and every sentence must build towards it.' – Edgar Allan Poe

For most of the last century, the short story writer had a ready market for his work, thanks to the many periodicals on both sides of the Atlantic which were willing to publish them. Most of these have faded into history now, and although there are plenty of websites which will publish short fiction, they usually pay little or nothing for it. Yet while the outlets for short story collections have reduced, there still seems to be a market out there. And from the writer's point of view, short is beautiful, because it is so much less demanding – except that while one good idea may make a novel, you're going to need ten or twelve to make a book of short stories.

Collections of twist-in-the tale stories in the tradition of Roald Dahl can do well (though he set a high benchmark), as can horror, the supernatural and science fiction. Inventiveness is key; writing an effective story is a knack. But you do need to present a collection that hangs together. It won't work if you try to mix twist-in-the-tale yarns with sci fi tales, out-and-out horror with ghost stories or romance with soft porn, because in each case you'd be trying to sell to two different groups of readers. A common theme for your stories is a good idea, and will help in marketing the book – perhaps they are all about marital strife, or trouble over money, or the workplace.

If you've written one great short story, don't expect a publisher to be interested, not yet. You can't bind a 5000-word story into a book (it would be horribly thin, or the type would have to be stupidly large). If you have managed to write a story you're proud of, see if you can follow it up with another, and another, until you have a total of 40,000 words or more. Now you might have a book worth marketing.

CHAPTER 6

Fantasy, ghost stories and science fiction

It's clear that a lot of people who launch themselves into writing in these genres have abandoned the basic requirement of the novelist to be original. Science fiction fans and Tolkienists may get away with this, to an extent; the sales figures for works in these categories indicate that even highly-derivative stories can find followers if the adventures are well told and the settings exciting and compelling.

Nevertheless, exactly the same rules apply. Your characters should be people, not caricatures or clichés. That means they must be believable; neither too fearless and heroic (the goodies) nor too unremittingly evil (the baddies).

The story too has to be credible – you need to be able to suspend disbelief. Fantastic and impossible things may happen, but they must follow a consistent set of rules. Look at *Gulliver's Travels*; the basic idea of the main part of the story, that a man travelling the world might come across lands where the people are vastly bigger or smaller than he is, is plain ludicrous, and would have been equally so in the early 18th century. But it's an entrancing novel, thanks in large part to Swift's considerable skill at story-telling, and it has been reprinted (and more recently filmed) down the ages. It would have gone wrong, however, if Swift had continued to pile improbability upon improbability. As it is, everything that happens in each section of the book is a logical outcome from just one whopping improbability. In the first part the writer explores the question: what would happen if a normal human encountered a race of otherwise normal people who are only six inches tall? Gulliver is an early example of a high-concept story – one based on a simple big idea.

If you're writing sci fi or fantasy you will have to work at your settings, because unlike authors of conventional fiction, you won't be able to write 'a wet Saturday morning in Oxford Street' and leave the rest to the reader's imagination. I have seen many submissions which failed to invoke any sense of place. You read a few paragraphs and find yourself thinking, *Where the hell are we? What does this place look like?* The author needs to develop a clear idea of the setting before starting to write.

Fantasy

It's difficult to escape from the shadow of Tolkien in tackling fantasy fiction. Truth is, I'm not sure your readers will want you to. Just try to make your world, your people, different from his, in an interesting, credible way. You might try making them closer to real life. One of the reasons *The Lord of the Rings* works so well is that hobbits (and most of the other characters, at least the goodies) are so very close to ordinary humans, and the country in which the story plays out is so very close to Britain, except it's a Britain where the geography has been rearranged, transport has never got beyond the horse (and of course, magic reigns).

A few thoughts:

A compelling **setting** is key. What makes Tolkien's work so absorbing to his fans is that he created an entire world, complete with languages. You have the feeling that the author could tell you far more about the world of Middle Earth than there is room for in *The Lord of the Rings* (as of course he could). So in creating your setting, do it properly. Design it alongside your characters.

The further away the **characters** in fantasy and science fiction are from humanity, the harder they are to care about. It's all very well making one of your characters a goblin, a robot or a half-man, half-dragon, but don't then follow it with a half-dragon/half-goblin, a half-robot/half-frog/half-mushroom and a thing that looks a bit like a tea cosy with legs (except for laughs). The reader will soon stop giving a damn about any of them. The same applies when you overdo the drama by introducing a new kind of monster to be slain on every other page. This can be dreadfully tedious. We simply stop caring.

Magic is as indispensable to fantasy fiction as chillis are to curries, but like chillis, it should be used sparingly. Too much magic would save the characters from having to think, or run, or fight, or hide, or anything else. So the rules governing its use must be as strict and as thoroughly policed as those governing firearms. Work out exactly what magic will make possible in your world and what it won't. Set the rules at the beginning, and don't allow them to change.

Portals still rule. At one stage I was planning to write that they have been done to death, but they work so well that I don't think they will ever be done to death. Nothing can quite compare with that moment when a character steps through the back of the wardrobe, or falls into the wormhole, or finds the key to the stargate, except possibly the moment when he can't get back.

Portals are everywhere, though you don't always recognise them. C S Lewis's wardrobe (*The Lion, The Witch and The Wardrobe*, 1950) is one of the great inventions of junior fiction, second only to the rabbit hole in *Alice In Wonderland*. Philip Pullman used invisible, temporary portals very cleverly and subtly in the *His Dark Materials* trilogy. The time machine in H G Wells' story of 1895 is a portal, the central image of the book. So is the locked door to Frances Hodgson Burnett's *The Secret Garden* (1911), although that is not a fantasy story. You could even argue that the gate at the bottom of Bilbo Baggins' garden is a kind of portal, as it marks a cut-off between the homely environment of the hobbits and the vast and much more terrifying world beyond.

So keep the portals coming, but make them original.

Ghost stories

The tradition behind the ghost story is firmly rooted in the golden years of the 19th and early 20th centuries, and although some excellent work is being written by modern masters and mistresses of the genre, it's noticeable that almost all modern TV and film adaptations are based on the old stories. You're going to have think outside the box to make a mark in this genre, but as ghost stories are such fun to write, I suggest you go right ahead. If your ideas are original and your stories chilling enough, you might find some readers.

I suspect that some people enjoy writing horror stories a little too much for their own good, and that of their readers. The creepier tales which arrive on my desk tend to suffer from a common failing – the nasty bits have been laid on with a trowel:

Amanda screamed in helpless, terrified horror as a ghastly apparition rose up to meet her from the foul-smelling depths of the stinking pit. As she screamed and desperately struggled to escape, her flimsy nightdress was torn from her slim, vulnerable body. The rotted, festering lips of the awful being were getting closer and she felt herself hopelessly trapped as if by some giant, evil power beyond the grave. The foul-smelling thing's slimy, claw-like fingers grasped her quivering flesh…

I get the impression that writers who produce this kind of stuff are simply getting off on writing, forgetting all about the poor old reader. Here is M R James, the master, at work:

A penwiper? No, no such thing in the house. A rat? No, too black. A large spider? I trust to goodness not – no. Good God! A hand like the hand in that picture!

In another infinitesimal flash he had taken it in. Pale dusky skin, covering nothing but bones and tendons of appalling strength; coarse, black hairs, longer than ever grew on a human hand; nails rising from the ends of the fingers and curving sharply down and forward…

- Canon Alberic's Scrapbook, Ghost Stories of an Antiquary (1904)

This is about as explicit as James gets. At least 95 per cent of the text of his stories is concerned with scene-setting, with the building up, little by little, of tension and expectation. By the time of the 'reveal', we are with James or his protagonist in the abandoned church, the neglected graveyard or the haunted library. Here is James himself on how it's done:

Two ingredients most valuable in the concocting of a ghost story are, to me, the atmosphere and the nicely managed crescendo... Let us, then, be introduced to the actors in a placid way; let us see them going about their ordinary business, undisturbed by forebodings, pleased with their surroundings; and into this calm environment let the ominous thing put out its head, unobtrusively at first, and then more insistently, until it holds the stage. – M R James, Ghosts and Marvels

Writers of supernatural fiction would do well to heed this advice.

Science fiction

Back in the innocent days when it was still possible that there might be little green men living on our planetary neighbours, sci fi was so rich in possibilities that you could do the fiction part without knowing any science at all. C S Lewis, who was very far from being a scientist, managed to write a wonderful novel about a man travelling to Mars and meeting aliens (*Out of the Silent Planet*, 1938) with no more technical detail than to say that the rocket which took him there used 'some of the lesser-known properties of solar radiation'. Today the technology of space travel (within the Solar System, at least) is highly developed and well publicised, and an author couldn't put anyone on board a rocket to Mars, Jupiter or anywhere else without doing a great deal of rather technical homework, unless he wanted the sci fi buffs to laugh all the way to the Star Trek Convention.

Another problem is that all the obvious story ideas have now been used so many times it's hard to wring anything new out of them. Journeys to the Moon and planets, messages from the stars, wormholes, time tunnels, extra dimensions, intergalactic war, hostile invaders, friendly invaders, getting lost in space, getting left behind in space, getting trapped in the past, getting trapped in the future – all done many times. So you need an ingenious mind, and a keen awareness of what NASA is up to, to dream up something that will please this particular market.

However, if you're the kind of person who wants to write science fiction, that may well describe you anyway. Sci fi is great fun to write, and the best stories focus on the human angle rather than the technology, so provided you do as Lewis did and keep the technical stuff to what you know so that you don't make the buffs collapse with laughter, I suggest you go right ahead.

Of course, humans don't have to be human. Even if your characters are three inches tall and look like cucumbers, they will still have feelings, urges, fears, motives, successes and failures, friends and enemies. You are quite free to set any of the conventional novel themes (love, war, betrayal, survival, redemption etc) in space, but please don't expect anyone to enjoy your story if the only nods to the setting are the plastic suits and the occasional throwaway line about being a hundred light years from Earth. People read sci fi to travel into space, or to have space come to them, not to watch East Enders with ray guns. I hope.

CHAPTER 7

Writing for children

Judging by the number of children's books we receive at Mereo, junior fiction is the most popular genre of all, at least among writers. And indeed the market is large and lucrative, with 10,000 new children's titles published in the UK each year, and the top-selling authors at both ends of the age range shifting copies by the freighterload; 30 million for Eric Carle's *The Very Hungry Caterpillar*, and 450 million for the Harry Potter series.

No wonder so many people are tempted to have a go. Well – it's easy to write for children, isn't it? You only need to come up with a couple of thousand words, less if it's for little ones, and you can do the drawings yourself...

The truth is that although it's great fun and seems relatively easy to write for children, making money from it is very difficult indeed. Only the most irresistible ideas, presented vividly and clearly, have a chance of capturing young imaginations when children (and their parents) have so much choice. I don't know how many kids' books are pouring from the pens and laptops of hopeful parents, aunts, grandfathers etc at this moment as I write, but I'd guess that in the UK alone it must be many tens of thousands.

And there's another snag, for any author who hasn't got the backing of a publisher – it may actually be more expensive to produce a thousand-word illustrated book for young children than a paperback novel with 100,000 words, because of the cost of illustration and colour reproduction.

Many children's books submitted to Mereo are too traditional, tending to be peopled by middle-class families and healthy, well-adjusted white children with big houses and green fields to roam in, and not a mobile phone or an iPod in sight. Very often they are about the adventures of a cute creature of some kind, a puppy, a baby elephant or a cuddly toy. This is usually because they have been written by older authors brought up in a more innocent era. I suspect that parents and grandparents remember the books they were weaned on and feel that the new generation ought to enjoy the same sort of stuff. A visit to a bookshop will soon show you how far the market has moved on.

Another mistake which many amateur authors seem to make is to forget the vital importance of pitching a book correctly at a particular age range. You have no chance of success if your story is written in adult style, with adult vocabulary, yet it's for and about seven-year-olds, or if you produce a 60,000-word novel about a kitten (yes, I've seen it done).

But, I hear you say, my kids LOVED my story! Well, that was probably because their mum/dad/granny created it just for them. They probably like the cut-out paper masks and the home-made ice lollies you make too, with all the colour and flavour settled at the bottom. Other people's children (and their parents), and publishers, will be harsher judges.

Many people submit a story for young children which is either unillustrated or adorned with amateur sketches by the author, or a close relative who happens to be clever at drawing. It's possible that a publisher will see the potential in your idea and commission a professional to do the job properly, but please don't assume your own, or your daughter's, drawings will be good enough to appear in a trade-published book. If you're self-publishing you're likely to need professional illustration to have a realistic chance of a book for the under-tens being accepted by the trade, and that costs a lot of money – way into four figures. Most of the books on the shelves of the stores have been printed by the containerload in far-off countries such as Poland and China, which is the only way of making them affordable in the shops. On a small print run in the UK your costs are likely to dictate a cover price which is far too high for the market. This is why only a tiny few of the most original and entertaining children's books will ever sell in any quantity.

But, having said that, if you still want to try to write a successful children's book, here are some suggestions.

The basic requirements

The golden rules for writing children's fiction are the same as they are for adults. You need an original, compelling protagonist; a boy who lives in a cardboard box, a girl who can't stop growing, a family who travel everywhere on roller skates.

Then you need to give your hero a challenge, a problem, something that is getting in the way of everything else. The story, of course, will be about overcoming it; it might involve finding a lost pet, getting to see Santa at the North Pole or standing up to the bullies in the playground. Once again we come back to the essential triangle of character, objective and obstacle.

Now target it properly. Decide just which child you are writing for, and fix him or her in your mind as you write. You can't expect a five-year-old to enjoy a story about football, or a twelve-year-old to care about magical toys. The book needs to be all of a piece. Picture books for tinies will contain a thousand words or less, laid out very clearly in biggish type, and the pictures must be excellent. At the other extreme, a novel for the sub-teens can be much longer, 50,000 words or more (the longest Potter book, *Harry Potter and the Order of the Phoenix*, was 257,000) but it still has to be rooted in the reader's world and to talk about concepts which matter to children of that age.

A few key points:

- As with an adult book, try to hook the reader with the first paragraph.

- Don't be too didactic or moralistic. Children don't like being lectured to; they get enough of that at school. That doesn't mean to say your story can't show your character learning and improving through experience.

- Use plenty of dialogue, but keep it short and punchy.

- Try to entertain – children love to be made to laugh.

■ Never talk down to children. Immerse yourself as far as you can in their world, their thoughts, fears, dreams and hopes.

■ Don't write in rhyme, except possibly for tinies – publishers don't like it.

On writing by children

'I know I was writing stories when I was five. I don't know what I did before that. Just loafed, I suppose.' – P G Wodehouse

At Mereo, we sometimes get submissions from authors who turn out to be still at school. Some of these books are remarkably accomplished, and we have published one or two, once they have received the attentions of a sympathetic editor.

Talented authors seem to start young. The most famous child's novel has to be Daisy Ashford's *The Young Visiters*, written in 1890 when the author was nine. Its charm comes from an inventive story and sympathetic characters, as well as its erratic spelling and punctuation and a great deal of unintended humour ('I shall put some red ruge on my face said Ethel because I am very pale owing to the drains in this house'). The American actress Ally Sheedy wrote a best-selling story about a mouse when she was twelve.

It's clear that the knack for writing develops at an early age, like the gift for being able to imitate accents or remember tunes. I have a hunch these skills are connected; something to do with the rhythm and musicality of good prose, a love of words and the sounds they make. The limitations youthful writers experience are not usually to do with putting words together successfully, or with vocabulary or the skill of description or handling direct speech; indeed they often seem to excel instinctively at matters which defeat many older authors. Their failings are usually connected simply with their lack of experience of the world. They are on safe ground in describing the doings of people their own age, but their accounts of adult behaviour tend to lack realism; the police give young children jobs as crime fighters, a bank robber gives himself up in terror when faced with a boy and a puppy, a rich businessman keeps his money in gold coins. Young authors often forget about the physical limitations of their characters too, and have six-inch high elves eating apples and fish climbing ladders.

The lion looked at the time. It was nearly six o'clock. He wanted to catch the news to see if Manchester United had won the Cup Final.

The gaps in children's experience tend to show through when they try to describe how a business works or what parents say to one another, though they may also be brilliantly original. So books written by children are often marvels of achievement and off the scale in school gradecard terms, but proud parents setting out to invest in their child's talent should probably not expect too many sales to result. People buy children's books because they have been superbly written *for* ten-year-olds, not precociously written *by* them.

Of course, if you have a child who shows promise as a writer, you must not allow this to stop you from encouraging them in any way you can.

CHAPTER 8

How not to write poetry

'All poets write bad poetry. Bad poets publish them, good poets burn them' – Umberto Eco

We get lots of poetry collections sent to us at Mereo, mostly just intended for friends and family. Some of it is very good. We point out in our author information that while we don't expect to edit verse creatively, we do need to check through for hard errors, like spelling mistakes and misplaced punctuation. In doing so I often notice that a small change would help a line to scan – it might be something as simple as changing 'he is' to 'he's' – or I might spot a better rhyme, but when I make such suggestions I very often get a 'thanks, but no thanks'. Fair enough, it's your poem. And I am not a qualified poet. But then, who is?

I often feel, as with literary fiction, that the author of a poetry book would have benefited from reading more of the professionals' stuff. Many less accomplished poets are stuck with the notion that all verse has to rhyme, and go to extraordinary lengths to force it to do so, sometimes using quite the wrong word, because rhyming is apparently more important to them than meaning. The spirit of William McGonagall lives on.

I'm not knocking poetry that rhymes and scans – Pam Ayres has won a following of millions for hers – but her rhyming and scanning are spot on, and her poems are funny.

While most amateur poets understand rhyme, they often fail dismally when it comes to scansion, and this can make their work hard to read. But there is more of course to successful poetry than either. Most of the finest poetry does not rhyme or follow a rigid meter (though it usually does have rhythm). It just touches you; it has a way of ringing in your head, of reaching your soul. And it *sounds* good. Take the famous opening lines of *The Waste Land*, by T S Eliot:

April is the cruellest month, breeding
Lilacs out of the dead land, mixing
Memory and desire, stirring
Dull roots with spring rain.

It seems to me that while good poetry owes much to the rhythm, the ring and the cadence of words, above and beyond that it is about using language in ways that most of us would never have thought of, to put across original thoughts, ideas and images. I'd suggest it has two key dimensions – first it needs to have something interesting to say, as opposed to a popular amateur theme like 'isn't the garden lovely in spring', and secondly it needs to say it in a powerful, original way, devoid of cliché, using unexpected yet effective words and word associations.

Let's start with a typical piece of verse on the above topic by an imaginary not-very-good amateur poet:

> *In my back garden in springtime many flowers are found,*
> *Daffodils, roses and anemones abound,*
> *Such happiness do they give us, so vibrant and gay,*
> *While the birds they are singing, the blackbird and the jay.*

How can we make it better? There is certainly room for improvement. Let's start with the basics of conventional poetry by tweaking the words a little to help it to scan (and while we're at it, let's ditch those useless commas):

> *In my garden in spring many flowers are found*
> *Daffodils, roses and snowdrops abound*
> *Such joy do they give us, so vibrant and gay*
> *While the birds they are singing, the blackbird and jay.*

Now let's make a couple of changes to make the poem more truthful to nature, and tidy up that clumsy 'joy do they' and 'birds they are':

> *In my garden in spring many flowers are found*
> *Daffodils and snowdrops bring life to the ground*
> *Such pleasure they give us, so vibrant and gay*
> *While the wild birds are calling, the blackbird and jay.*

It's neat enough now, but still vacuous. How about:

In my garden in spring many flowers abound
Daffodils and snowdrops push life from the ground
Their short days are numbered, so cruel is the spring
The earth will reclaim them as summer takes wing.

At last, the poet has made a point, even if it's not a very original one. There's even a metaphor – the summer is compared to a bird. But what would a more 'serious' poet make of this subject? Chances are he or she would forget about rhyming and find some more interesting words, along with extensive use of simile and metaphor:

In my garden in spring, spiteful April rain
Drowns the bare soil beneath my boots.
Under the wall, old leaves lick the grey bones of the trellis.
In the sward under the euonymus, celandines shine
Innocent as choirboys.
March has given them life; they do not know that May will
murder them.

If those lines aren't particularly good, they are at least much better than the first example. At least they have something to say. Better still, no one else has written them, and they never will.

So if this is you I'm talking about, try to think of something interesting to say, if you want others to appreciate your poems, and to say it in words which are not the obvious ones. When you think you have finished, go through the poem looking for anything which looks remotely like a cliché – and that could mean any place where you've put words together predictably, like 'rolling hills' or 'the rain hammers down' – and ask yourself if your poem wouldn't be improved by substituting something more surprising. 'Flat hills' may seem an oxymoron, but maybe you see them that way because of your mood. That would be much more revealing.

Incidentally I can recommend a very useful site at www.rhymezone.com the next time you're struggling to find a rhyme for 'ecumenical'.

PART TWO

HOW NOT TO WRITE THE TEXT

CHAPTER 9

Tackling the manuscript

Gather your ingredients

If you're writing fiction, proceed as outlined in chapters 5 and 6. If you're writing a factual book about a particular topic, your preparation will be more about assembling and sorting information. Start by writing out a contents list, with working chapter titles. This will soon define the topics you need to cover, identify any glaring gaps and enable you to start putting the book into a coherent order.

Let's say you're writing a history of wine. Your contents list might look, in broad outline, like this:

Dedication (if you want).

Foreword – perhaps contributed by a wine expert you know.

Acknowledgements – to anyone who helped you or gave you permission to use material

Introduction – what this book is about, why you wrote it, who it's for.

Chapter 1 – Ancient history – the first traces of wine-making in the Middle East etc

Chapter 2 – All about grapes

Chapter 3 – The Romans

Chapter 4 – France

…and so on. At the end you might want to add some appendices, such as maps of the world's wine regions, a list of the best claret vintages or a run-down of grape varieties. (See chapter 15 for more about the parts of a book.) You will probably also want to add a bibliography, with the titles of books you have used and those recommended for further reading. And you may well need an index, also covered in chapter 15.

Research

Once you've got the above written down, you have a plan. You will probably find it helps to prepare your contents page on a separate file so that you can keep it open on your PC and coordinate changes between the contents list and the main manuscript (by the way, having two monitors so that you can view two documents or web pages at the same time is a huge help in sorting information between files – once my teenage son had shown me how to do it, I wondered how I had ever managed without).

I have found that the best and most natural approach for

me is to start with a skeleton of the book, as indicated above, and then build the text upon it piece by piece, rather than working through from the beginning to the end. Information will come to you from a variety of sources, and you may find, for example, that a book about the history of Mediterranean culture yields material about the origins of the corkscrew as well as the derivation of the various grape varieties. Work your way through one source book at a time, marking useful passages with those sticky coloured tabs you can buy from stationers – you might colour-code them, so purple stickers relate to grape varieties, red to France, green to the New World etc. You can type up the information into the right chapter as you go. Gradually the text under each chapter heading will grow, and your book will start taking shape. Somewhere along the way you might realise that you need an additional chapter, say on modern wine chemistry, or perhaps there is so little to say about one topic that it's best to abandon the idea of giving it a chapter of its own and add it somewhere else.

The Internet has made researching a book ridiculously easy. The problem with this is that everyone else can do it just as quickly and easily as you can, so rather than rewrite what Wikipedia has to say about, for example, Château Haut Brion, you might as well tell your readers to look it up themselves. Internet references quickly become old hat, particularly funny quotes, and wrong or confusing information is sometimes copied from website to website. So use the net, but do try to find original material in places which surfing cannot reach. Old books and newspapers are prime sources, and the British Library is one of the greatest seats of knowledge in the world, with a treasure trove of around 14 million books and well over 100 million periodicals, plus countless historical documents

(OK, I got that from Wikipedia). If you think *Decanter* magazine might have written about a topic you're researching in September 1976, you just need to register with the BL, take the underground to St Pancras, fill in a request form and an assistant will serve the relevant issue up to you a short while later.

Do make sure you consult the books which have been written before on your subject, if any – not so much to use material from them (which is perfectly OK as long as you put it in your own words, and where appropriate acknowledge it) as to make sure you have not missed anything important and are not making any stupid mistakes.

People, of course, are the most valuable source of all, and one person who's in the know will often pass you on to two or three more who can help you, and so on. I've already dealt with biographies, but interviews with people who were there are useful for titles in other genres too – books about music, the theatre, sport, business and many more.

Chapter headings and other matters

Novels are often presented with numbered chapters only, but factual books nearly always need named chapters. They should be kept informative while you're developing the MS ('Storage, cellars and containers' rather than 'A twist of the corkscrew'), otherwise you might forget what you intended to cover in each. If your book is designed to entertain, not just to provide authoritative information, you should try to make sure the chapter titles will make the book appear a good read. Interesting chapter titles will help to sell your book, because people will browse the contents before buying, and dull, dry titles imply a dull, dry book. A witty book needs witty chapter titles, while a dramatic story needs titles which enthral and engage ('A light in the darkness' would be better than 'The development of astronomical telescopes' - or you could use the latter as a sub-heading). A good editor will suggest some more interesting chapter titles for you if it's not your forte.

Many authors of factual books in particular like to add little quotations from poets, politicians and the like at the heads of the chapters (correctly called epigraphs). This works well, as long as they are appropriate and likely to be new to most readers – if they are quotes most of us have seen many times before, they will suggest that the author is a bore or a dunce and what follows will not be worth reading.

CHAPTER 10

How to use dialogue

I'm devoting two chapters to dialogue, because good use of the spoken word and the correct handling of it on the page are critical, and very few people manage dialogue correctly; in fact I often have to rewrite it. From the way it's rendered in some manuscripts I have seen, I've wondered if the author has ever seen a novel, let alone read one. Even writers with an otherwise excellent command of prose make basic errors in dialogue which severely hobble their attempts at conveying conversation.

Non-fiction writers need to know how to handle dialogue just as novelists do; the rules are the same, except that with non-fiction you will be reporting the truth, or at least a fair representation of it.

The purpose of dialogue

In a novel (or a factual story, for that matter), dialogue has three main purposes:

1 Moving the story on:

'It was you who switched the letters, wasn't it Roger? Well, I'm leaving you!'

2 Providing background information which will be relevant to your story, for example about people, settings or recent events:

'Now this is the original kitchen. It was closed off when the old squire died. The house has been empty since then, unfortunately. We're only a small village and there's not much to attract new blood here, at least there wasn't until they built the new housing estate…'

No doubt a few chapters on we'll be hearing about the young woman who has inherited this house, or what the people from the new housing estate get up to at night, or what happens in the house when darkness falls.

3 Revealing character:

'We are just going, Captain Segura,' Wormold said.

 'Nonsense. You are my guest. It is only just after midnight.'

 Wormold's sleeve caught a glass. It fell and smashed, like the birthday party. 'Waiter, another glass.' Segura began to sing softly, 'The rose I plucked in the garden,' leaning towards Milly, turning his back on Dr Hasselbacher.

Milly said, 'You are behaving very badly.'

'Badly? To you?'

'To all of us. This is my seventeenth birthday party, and it's my father's party, not yours.'

'Your seventeenth birthday? Then you must certainly be my guests. I'll invite some dancers to our table.'

'We don't want any dancers,' Milly said.

Our Man In Havana, Graham Greene (1958)

This exchange reveals in a few lines the awkward, retiring nature of Wormold (Milly's father and the novel's protagonist), the controlling, lecherous personality of Captain Segura, the police chief, and the spirited confidence of young Milly.

Any chunk of dialogue which does not contribute to story, background or character should be deleted; it's just dead weight.

Here's another passage which does all three of these jobs, from that wonderful comic novel *Cold Comfort Farm*. Flora Poste (whose reforming zeal owes something to Jane Austen's *Emma* in the novel of the same name) is staying with her rustic cousins, the Starkadder family, and has embarked on a mission to rid them of their rural prejudices and foibles and bring them into the 20th century. In this passage, she realises that the handsome Seth has a future in Hollywood:

"You must tell me all about your work some time. What do you do on the evenings when you aren't – er – eating people?"

"I goes over to Beershorn" replied Seth, rather sulkily. The dark flame of his male pride was a little suspicious of having its leg pulled.

"To play darts?"

"No. I goes to the talkies."

Something in the inflection which Seth gave to the last word of his speech caused Flora to put down her sewing and glance up at him. Her gaze rested thoughtfully on his irregular but handsome features.

"The talkies, do you? Do you like them?"

"Better nor anything in the whoal world," he said fiercely. "Better nor my mother nor this farm nor Violet down at the vicarage, nor anything."

"Indeed," mused his cousin, still eyeing his face thoughtfully. "That's interesting. Very interesting indeed."

…Flora nodded, displaying courteous interest, but showing nothing of the plan which had suddenly occurred to her.

Cold Comfort Farm, Stella Gibbons (1932)

Making dialogue interesting

Unfortunately a great deal of dialogue, in novels which are not of the high standard required to succeed in today's market, is dull; just conventional chit-chat and exchange of information. The characters say ordinary things in ordinary ways using ordinary words; one answers a question, the other answers it. As mentioned above, not only is that boring, it isn't how people talk. Real people frequently talk at cross-purposes, misunderstand or fail to listen to one another, change the subject, repeat themselves or struggle for the right words. You can use all that very entertainingly to develop the characters in your story.

So try to flesh out your people and entertain the reader at the same time by doing more with your dialogue. Have your characters express themselves in original, interesting, witty or unintentionally entertaining ways (always consistent, of course, with their personalities and backgrounds). You can achieve this by becoming a collector of real-life dialogue. Listen to the way people talk, and when they say amusing, revealing or original things, note them discreetly down for future use.

Telling the story through dialogue

I don't want to lean too heavily on other authors, and (as will be mentioned in chapter 12) there are limits to how much you should quote from someone else's work without permission, so I'm going to use the following extract from an unpublished (in fact unfinished and untitled) novel of my own to show you how dialogue can be used to carry a story forward. Our hero, Patrick, is an innocent young man who has travelled to Scotland in vain pursuit of the girlfriend who has dumped him.

"Men always make the same mistake," said Stella, pouring more gin into her tonic. "You all think that if a woman agrees to go out with you and laughs at your jokes and complies with you in the bedroom occasionally, all you have to do is turn up every other evening and she'll go on loving you for ever. But that, my dear, is nowhere near enough."

"Yes, I know. They want you to remember birthdays and things. Buy them flowers. Tell them you love them. Send them cards with little poems on them. Is that what you mean?"

"Oh *Patrick*! It's more, my darling, much more than that." She leaned forward and the cleavage made its first appearance of the evening. "She wants your attention. She wants your *complete* attention. She wants you to make her feel that she is the only woman in the room and that for you, she will always be the only woman in the room. Test question now. Have you ever upset her by looking at another woman?"

"Very rarely. I mean, three or four times at most."

"Aha! Give me one example. Truthfully."

"Well, there was this girl at a New Year drinks party I went to with her. She was very" – Patrick tried to use eyes and hands to indicate what he meant without the crudity that would have been appropriate in male company – "well built, and she was wearing – a sort of purple vest three sizes too small, and very high heels, and not much else."

"And how long did you spend looking at her?"

"Oh not long, only a few seconds at a time. And she was looking back. I mean, all the men were looking at her. Even some of the women said they wished they had her figure. She was a real stunner. It was OK, Anna said she understood. We joked about it afterwards, but she was really off with me when we went to bed."

"That is so sad." Stella shook her head slowly. "Such a wonderful opportunity, and you wasted it. You silly, silly boy." It was the first time she had used the 'b' word, but Patrick had feared it was coming.

"Oh, I'd never have done anything. I do love Anna. I really fancy Anna. More than I fancied the girl in the purple vest."

"Darling, that is not what I mean. This girl in the purple vest gave you a heaven-sent opportunity to show Anna that she is the only woman for you. If you'd only had the guts and the common sense to ignore the little tart and look only at Anna" – Stella demonstrated this for a moment by holding Patrick's gaze steadfastly with her cool blue eyes – "look *only* at her, all the time you were there, while every other chap was ogling the vest, and then when she said "what do you think of that girl in the purple vest?" you had said "which girl?" and looked around as if you hadn't realised there was anyone else in the room, do you know something?"

"Well? Tell me."

"You would still be together."

"I see." Patrick's face fell.

"Do you really see? Because you must understand, Patrick, all women, even the truly beautiful ones, the ones who look like Elizabeth Taylor, or Audrey Hepburn – *especially* the beautiful ones – all women are terrified that they might be ugly." She tried to pull an ugly face, with limited success. "The woman you love has to be told she is beautiful. *She* has to know it, not just you. *Make* her know it, Patrick!"

"I will. I really will. Oh God." Patrick felt crushed. "Do you think it's too late?"

"I don't know. Maybe not. It depends…" a long pause.

"What does it depend on?"

"It depends on how much she really loves you. And on whether there's someone else in the wings."

"Oh, no. No chance. No one else. She made a point of saying so in the note. She didn't have to say so if it wasn't true, because she was leaving me anyway." He felt on firm ground here.

"She actually mentioned it in a note? Tell me what it said, exactly."

"It said 'there is no one else, so please don't imagine there is'."

Stella rolled her eyes, drew vigorously on her cigarette, downed the rest of her gin and tonic and put a hand on Patrick's. He noticed that she had very long and elegant fingers.

"It may be too late, my darling," she said. "You and I are going to have to work fast."

This sets us up for the next scene back in London, in which we discover that Anna does indeed have someone else in the wings.

Once you have the knack of writing good dialogue, you can tell a large part of your story with it. So learn to listen to your characters, and when you can hear them, start trusting them to tell your story for you.

CHAPTER 11

Dialogue - the rules

There is a subtle but clearly-defined code to reproducing dialogue on the printed page, and if you fail to follow it, you will leave your readers floundering. The rules for handling speech in English text are universally understood, or should be, and you will see them demonstrated in most professionally-published books. And yes, we do need rules – without them you are plunging your reader into a fog of anarchy and confusion.

First, place an inverted comma (quotation mark/speech mark) at the beginning and end of each passage of quoted words. Traditionally double speech marks are used, but single ones will do fine. I'll come to the purpose of having two kinds shortly. If the whole sentence is in quotes, the closing inverted comma comes after the full stop.

Start a new paragraph each time the speaker changes, but don't start a new one if the same speaker is continuing, unless it's a very long speech. If that's the case, start the new paragraph with a quotation mark but do NOT put a closing quotation mark at the end of the previous one – this is to show that the same person is continuing to speak.

Contrary to the belief of a surprising number of new authors, there is no rule that says you should start a new paragraph every time you open quotes – in fact it can look absurd:

She turned to him and said,
'We're going to have to sort this out'.

You don't need a 'said' if the quotes are preceded by a few words which make it clear who's speaking:

Andrew turned. 'I very much doubt it, Patricia.'

But you will need to start a new paragraph after the quoted words, assuming that's the end of Andrew's speech.

Something else to be avoided is the clumsy and unnecessary double speech tag:

"For God's sake stop whingeing, Carl," said Crispian. "We're at a party and it's a damn good one too," he added.

Many amateur writers of fiction seem to feel readers will know who is speaking without being told. Not so – I often see passages in which it is difficult or impossible to identify the speakers. You must never let the reader embark on a line of quoted text without first making it clear who is speaking. You may make an exception if words come out of the blue:

'So this is what you've been up to!'
Celia spun round to see Tom's grinning face in the doorway.

Even after you have been talking about a particular character and follow it with a statement from them, you should label it with a 'said Fred', 'added Jim' etc (a speech tag). The only exception is a two-part dialogue where it's obvious the speakers are alternating. If it's a long dialogue, you still need to remind the reader from time to time who is speaking by inserting a 'said Fred'. Put the speech tag in after the first quoted sentence or phrase – don't leave it until the end of a long statement. For example, 'Let's go' said Fred. 'We can always come back tomorrow and tidy up our tools…'

If the quote ends in a full stop, exclamation mark or question mark, there should be no full stop after the closing quotation mark.

Remember that your purpose is to make your dialogue jump off the page and into the reader's head without her ever having to stop to work out who's talking. Follow these rules, and your readers will not even notice your punctuation. Break them and you'll soon have them scratching their heads.

Incidentally, quotation marks are definitely not used on notices, advertisements and the like. I suppose the chap who wrote "PLEASE DON'T PARK HERE!" reasoned that as the words had been said by someone, ie himself, they constituted a kind of quotation, so they needed to be in quote marks.

The following extract from a recent Mereo title demonstrates several of the rules of good direct speech management. Note how the paragraphing and the association of quoted words with the unquoted words next to them makes it clear at every point who is speaking, despite the fact that four characters are present.

"I won't hold you up," Zawutu said. "Just wanted to say goodbye once more and thank you for everything." His eyes were on Hawthorn.

"And may I add my thanks to that," Ingabe said, reaching out a hand in Hawthorn's direction.

"I'll get on board, Alistair," Humphries said sensitively. "Don't be too long. Goodbye again, Mr President, Mr Ingabe." He saluted and walked up the ramp into the aircraft.

Zawutu turned to Hawthorn. "Well, Alistair. Take care. Off you go now. Oh, by the way. I've had new maps printed and there's a certain hill guarding the entrance to the Impolo Valley which now and for always will be known after you."

Hawthorn laughed. "I just hope it never again has to fulfil the role of bottle stopper. Goodbye, sir." He saluted and turned up the ramp.

Hawthorn's Hill, Denis Redmond (Mereo, 2014)

Certain conventions in written English should be kept out of direct speech. Punctuation in particular should be very simple. Brackets look ridiculous – how do you voice a bracket? Ditto the colon and semi-colon, which just don't work when spoken. Nor do phrases in quote marks, as there is no audio version of an inverted comma. They are not exactly wrong, but they will make your dialogue a little more wooden and a little less realistic. The same applies to the use of the subjunctive tense ('If only I were younger'). Nor should you use numbers in direct speech, particularly quantities – it should be 'I ordered three pounds of potatoes', not 3lb.

If you suffer from punctuation diarrhoea – using two or more exclamation marks for emphasis, combining exclamation marks with question marks or typing long trails of dots or gratuitous capitals – please take the appropriate medication. They have no verbal counterpart and will make you look inarticulate and slightly crazy.

You need to make a clear distinction between words which are thought and those which are spoken. You can write 'he thought, "I wonder how I'm going to explain the hole in the ceiling"', but a more subtle and elegant way of doing it is to put the words which are thought in italics, without quotes: *How on earth am I going to explain that hole in the ceiling?* Better still, use internal monologue (see Chapter 5) – how on earth was he going to explain the hole in the ceiling?

'Said' says it all

'I've come to see Captain Macfarlane,' I stated.
'Can I help you, sir?' queried the young secretary.
'You already have,' I ventured to remark.
'I'm sorry' she apologised.
'Come any nearer and I'll shoot,' he warned.

I hope those examples demonstrate why you should resist the temptation to try endless substitutes for 'said' just to avoid repetition. It's ugly and unnecessary, and taken to extremes it becomes ludicrous, to the point where all the reader will notice is your word, sitting there playing gooseberry between your lines of dialogue, yet so many inexperienced authors do it.

'Never use a verb other than 'said' to carry dialogue. The line

of dialogue belongs to the character; the verb is the writer sticking his nose in. But 'said' is far less intrusive than grumbled, gasped, cautioned, lied.' – Elmore Leonard

'"Said" is a convention so firmly established that readers for the most part do not even see it. This helps to make the dialogue realistic by keeping the superstructure invisible.' – How Not To Write A Novel, *Sandra Newman and Howard Mittelmark*

Quite. Similarly, don't make your characters suggest, comment, utter, reiterate, urge, advise, confirm, emphasise, taunt, speculate, tease, clarify, conclude or challenge. The quoted words themselves should tell the reader all he needs to know. And don't even consider using words which don't even *mean* speech, like consider, procrastinate, check, realise, defend, wonder, nod, shrug, smile, doubt, frown and reflect. Yes, all these and more I have seen authors use instead of simply 'said'.

Likewise, skip the adverbs, if the spoken words make them redundant:

'Thank you,' he said gratefully.

'Come here now!' she snapped commandingly.

'I expect dodging your local fan club must be quite exhausting for you,' said Annabel sarcastically.

Words which describe the style of speech, like 'grunted', 'whispered', 'chuckled' and 'screeched', are legitimate, as they add information about the voice itself.

Authors of high-flown fantasy fiction of the sub-Tolkien kind, or historical fiction, may still prefer to use words like 'proclaimed' and 'vowed'. Their readers probably won't mind.

How people don't talk

Now to that thorny question of 'ear':

'The Loch Ness Monster, a huge aquatic reptile said to be of the plesiosaur genus and an ancient legend in these Scottish glens, has long been sought by scientists who seek to prove its existence or otherwise, ye ken,' confided Angus, taking another sip of his Glenbogie.

'In the unlikely eventuality of a proven recent sighting, would the authorities not take all reasonable steps to obtain forensic evidence?' I queried, frowning.

'We are all severely traumatised by this near-death experience and need medical attention, followed by sleep and shelter for the rest of the night.'

'I could lose myself in your tender embrace, Caroline.'
'My feelings for you are of a reciprocal nature.'

I have changed the above examples, but I have not exaggerated them.

Given that most of us have conversations with other people every day of our lives from the age of about two, I confess myself mystified by the failure of some authors to notice that people never, ever talk like any of the people above unless they are trying to be funny. If you wish to be a writer of readable fiction, take time to listen to the speech of those talking around you, or to you, or indeed to the words coming out of your own mouth in reply, and imagine how the conversation would look when transcribed. You will quickly realise, if you haven't already, that most of us speak in fragments (verbless chunks), with pauses and repetition – we do not use concise, well-constructed sentences, conditional clauses, awkward tenses or abbreviations. No one says 'I will telephone you at 9 am after speaking to our production manager', they say 'I'll call you in the morning when I've had a word with Tom'. At the same time, people talk differently from each other; men talk differently from women, middle-aged men from young ones, factory workers from office managers, artists from engineers. I've seen quite a few amateur novels in which all the characters are equally articulate and all use the same vocabulary.

If you too are guilty of writing dialogue that's as wooden as Sherwood Forest, how can you knock it into shape? By *listening*, as mentioned above, to the way real people put sentences together, then by trying to make your invented conversations more succinct and a little more interesting.

'I hope you do not feel that last night I took advantage of a situation which may have been too difficult for you to escape from.'

'I think that I willed this encounter as much as you did, Henry. You need not fear any dominance by yourself.'

Everything about this passage is hopelessly stilted and formal, even for a 19th century romance, but it's based on an extract from a modern novel. This would do the job far better, and in far fewer words:

'I hope you don't feel I took advantage of you last night.'
'No, Henry. I wanted you as much as you wanted me.'

You could go further:

'Listen, about last night…'
'Don't worry, it's OK.' She grinned. 'It takes two, you know.'

In context, those few words tell us all we need to know: he's worried he might have gone too far after a few drinks; he didn't.

A sure sign that the writer has not listened to the way people talk is the failure to use elision in 'I am', 'we do not', 'you have' and so on. No one does that, unless they are putting the emphasis on the verb or the 'not' – 'But Luke, I *am* your father!' or 'I did *not* have sexual relations with that woman'. When writing natural direct speech it's best to keep to 'I'm', 'you've' and so on.

Having said all that, don't try to be *too* naturalistic – you don't want your dialogue to read like a transcript of a court hearing. Real people repeat themselves, ramble, waffle, pause and fill the gaps with ers and ums, but in books this would be boring and unreadable. Your aim is to distil the conversation down to what you need to say. The words spoken should reflect the personality and mood of the speaker, and convey the necessary information to move the story forward.

Don't try to use direct speech to deal with a long factual argument or explanation. It's much better to say (if you have to), 'He explained that the beams from the collider would be accelerated via a ring of magnets to a speed of 99 per cent of the speed of light, reaching a speed of five trillion electron volts…' Put this kind of stuff in a character's mouth and you'll turn the poor chap into the biggest bore on God's green Earth.

If you must insist on rendering a foreign or regional accent, please minimalise it, with just enough dropped aitches or slurred diphthongs to tell us that the speaker is, for example, a Yorkshireman or that his first language is French. Passages in full dialect are dreadfully tedious to read.

If a character's first language is not English, please don't try to get this across by sprinkling his speech with 'ciao, signora', or 'mais oui, monsieur'. If the fellow could deliver the rest of his message in English, you'd think he would also know the English words for hello and yes. Again, it's down to ear. The thinking writer listens to the way different kinds of real people talk and stores it up for later use.

What's gone wrong here?

She comes from a rich family and is constantly pampered.
I'm starving and could eat a horse.
I'm not afraid and am confident of victory.
With time, hopefully I will regain their full use.

I hope it's as obvious to you as it is to me that no normal person would say any of these things, yet my models for the above were all written by would-be novelists. Here's how they ought to read:

She comes from a rich family. She's pampered constantly.
I'm starving. I could eat a horse.
I'm not afraid. I'm sure we're going to win.
I hope I'll be able to use them again in time.

In three of those examples, the key to making them more natural is to use the smallest quantum of ink you can put on paper; the full stop. Listen to how people talk, and imagine where the full stops go. I think that may help you to work out how to phrase statements more naturally.

'I've known Patrick for a little over ten years, even before his successful debut on the London stage, yet he remains as unaware of his considerable acting ability as of his attraction to the fairer sex. Our Lancashire lad has matured into a man only likely to achieve greater fame and success.'

A hundred years ago, with a few corrections, this might have passed for a believable line of dialogue; today, it is hopelessly indigestible. Try this:

'I've known Patrick for years, since long before he made it in the West End. Funny thing is, he still doesn't have a clue just how good an actor he is, any more than he realises that half the girls in London have got the hots for him. Our Lancashire lad's a big boy now, and you know something? He's going to get bigger.'

Too much information

'Darling, you must invite your younger brother Tarquin to the wedding, although he probably won't come because he is a hippy and doesn't approve of our conventional middle-class lifestyle."

In plays and films, almost all the information has to be imparted through dialogue, so you have to get your characters to fill in the background – what town we're in, how long a couple have been married and so on. In a novel, you can simply stick this down on the page as part of the narrative. So there is no call for anyone to talk like Tarquin's sister-in-law.

COMMON UNNATURAL USAGE AND THE NATURAL EQUIVALENT

UNNATURAL	**NATURAL**
We are, you have, he does not etc	We're, you've, he doesn't (unless the verb or the 'not' is a point of emphasis)
I read it while going to work.	I read it while I was going to work.
She is arriving today and will return tomorrow.	She's coming today. She'll be going back tomorrow.
It will help towards buying the cows we have wanted for years.	It'll help us to buy those cows. We've been wanting them for years.
We can produce it at very low prices due to the low cost of labour in Turkey.	We can make it very cheaply. Labour's dirt cheap in Turkey.
We increased the tolerance by .001".	We added an extra thou to the tolerance.
Julie, a qualified accountant, will attend to the books.	Julie's a qualified accountant. She'll look after the books.
I will speak to my boss Mr Jackson on my next visit to the office as he will know the answer.	I'll speak to my boss the next time I'm in the office. Mr Jackson will know the answer.

Some inexperienced writers will end a passage of dialogue by moving it into reported speech to provide an executive summary of what was discussed next: 'She went on tell him that Diggory had joined the army, he asked if she wanted to see the rose garden and she told him she was too busy…' This is just laziness, or impatience, and sounds as if the writer can't be bothered to finish the job. But more to the point, why include these details anyway? Abbreviate by cutting the dialogue rather than by tailing off into reported speech. You could simply end the scene by writing, 'Anyway, let me tell you about Diggory and the new rose garden'.

The perils of telepathy

I confess to having scratched my head a few times over fantasy or SF stories in which the characters communicate by telepathy, and the writer has failed to manage this successfully on paper. If they are thinking lines of dialogue to each other, how do you render this on paper? You can't use 'said' or the equivalent because they aren't speaking, and you can't use 'thought' because that would mean they were thinking to themselves rather than communicating. The best solution I can offer is to put the dialogue in italics without quote marks or speech tags – which means the conversation must be restricted to two people, or you'll find yourself in more trouble than a Dalek on an escalator.

CHAPTER 12

The small print

Now let's look at some of the little misusages, mistakes and misapprehensions which get in the way of good prose, and make it harder for readers to follow and understand.

Vocabulary

You don't need – or indeed want – the vocabulary of an Oxford professor of literature to write a great book. It's much more useful to have a ready command of the words a reasonably well-educated reader will appreciate and understand. Unnecessarily obscure words (ululate, saccade, jocose, nugatory and recrudescence are among those I recall seeing in texts recently) are little use in story-telling (except perhaps in dialogue, to demonstrate a character's intellect or pomposity), though they may well play a useful role in factual books. Long words will slow your reader down. If you use the wrong word, you will stop her in her tracks, and damage her trust in you and your book. So make sure you know the difference between alternate and alternative, incredible and incredulous, prevaricate and procrastinate, tortuous and torturous, fortunate and fortuitous and to flout and to flaunt. Lots of people don't. Even if you are quite sure of a word's meaning, ask yourself whether there isn't a more familiar one that would do just as well. Writing is communication, not showing off.

By far the best way to develop your vocabulary is to read the right authors – authors who will stretch you without leaving you scratching your head too often. Most readers will pass over words they're not sure about, but you're learning to be a writer, so look them up.

Overdoing the adjectives (and adverbs)

Barnaby's mellow expression was quickly replaced by a thunderous scowl as his dark eyes narrowed grimly into a dangerous and threatening stare.

Does this example (not exaggerated, by the way) indicate simply that the author loves adjectives and feels that it's a case of the more of them the merrier? I suspect the explanation for the above sentence is more subtle. When writers shovel words in like this, I think they are worrying that their nouns and verbs just aren't good enough on their own. They are like the cook who loses confidence in a dish and tries to compensate by adding more and more seasoning, or a woman who plasters herself with mascara and rouge in a vain attempt to make up for imagined cosmetic faults.

'Use adjectives as if they cost you a toenail' – Terry Pratchett

Some famous authors have spoken as if they believe all adjectives should be outlawed. Certainly they should be used sparingly, and each should be made to pay its way. Some amateur authors seem to go for the most obvious adjective every time, like contestants in 'Blankety Blank', that TV word-association show where you had to guess the word that was most likely to complete a sentence. Many nouns carry their own adjectives with them like unwanted baggage, and the unthinking author sprinkles his prose with silvery moons, sleek sports cars, greedy pigs and crisp banknotes. Yet in creative writing, the familiar and the obvious are the plain boring.

So like a cost-conscious business manager, ask yourself how hard each of your adjectives is working. Don't tell us the grass is green and the sky is blue. If the grass is brown and the sky is black, that's giving us something to think about. Otherwise, it's just grass and sky, and probably not worth mentioning at all.

Too much information

When the train arrived at the station we got into one of the carriages and sat down.

Well who'd have thought it. I bet you didn't see *that* coming. The whole sentence could have been deleted, the narrative resuming when the train is under way, or when it's arrived, depending on the next development in the story.

Replacing his cup in the saucer, Rex picked up the last of his scone and finished it. Then he put the plate to one side, wiping his fingers on the napkin, and signalled to Cynthia to pour him another cup of tea.

Sorry, I'm asleep already. This would be interesting if Rex was a gorilla. Otherwise, cut it out. And don't make the reader wait while your characters stop to enjoy a five-course meal. There has to be a good reason for you to describe a meal in any detail; one of the characters is a chef, or you are contrasting references to food with the horrors of what one of the diners has just done to the heroine's sister, or the meal is the occasion of the hero's dismissal from his stockbroking firm. Come to think of it, I can't think of any reason to describe a meal in detail in a novel, because even in these situations you would need no more than a few brief references to the food itself.

Tautology

He nodded his head in agreement.
He shrugged his shoulders.

What else can you nod, or shrug?

They exchanged romantic love letters.
He dropped an unexpected bombshell.
He was irate with anger.

You could hardly be irate with joy.

Common examples of tautology:

Our table was pre-booked
I'll just double-check
A solution to the problem
Dressed in his uniform
Could potentially
He passed successfully
It was situated on the site
In conjunction with
During the course of the day
On two separate occasions
Joined together
Work colleagues

Don't tell us what you're going to tell us

Andrew had both good news and bad to deliver...
She explained where she had seen the fox...

The above are wasted words, much as adverbs of speech like 'angrily', 'sarcastically', 'hesitantly' and so on are usually wasted, because the dialogue that immediately follows will tell us these things.

There's no need for the whole of a conversation to appear in your story; in fact it's almost certainly a bad idea. You don't have to tell us that before Jim sacked John, he invited him to come into his office, said hello, told him to sit down and asked him if he wanted a cup of coffee. At the end, you don't have to tell us that they said goodbye. Nor do you have to tell us that John left the room (or for that matter that he entered it). Such details should only be included if they help to explain what one of the characters was thinking or feeling. The offer of a cup of coffee might be used as a warning to the reader that something is wrong, a tension-builder, if we know that Jim does not usually offer coffee to junior employees. Think how films do it. It's entirely normal to open a scene when the encounter is already in progress and to finish it before they say goodbye; we don't see the character enter the room and then leave again, except in documentaries, if that doesn't add anything useful.

Clichés

I remember challenging my grammar school English teacher about clichés, because at the age of twelve I thought phrases like 'as strong as an ox' and 'eyes like a hawk' were highly satisfying similes and wanted to use them at every opportunity. Now that I'm older and have seen them a few thousand times, I can see his point. At exactly what stage a neat expression becomes a cliché is a matter of opinion, but authors who wish to be taken seriously should err on the side of caution.

Of course it isn't just phrases like 'vice-like grip', 'keen legal mind' and 'nerves of steel' which are clichés but situations – the switched glass of poison, the hero saved when the villain's gun clicks on an empty chamber, the girl waking in a hospital bed with memory loss after an ordeal, the man living alone coming home to pour out his troubles to his faithful dog/parrot/photo of dead wife. And characters can be clichés too – fiery redheads, fat, jolly uncles, the stereotypical gay best friend, the stolid country bumpkin. By all means stick a bumpkin in your novel if you want to, but make him different; make him *your* bumpkin. Give him one or two unbumpkinlike characteristics, such as a fear of mice or a passion for fine porcelain.

Storylines can be clichés, for that matter. So can whole books. Don't write one of those.

Misrelation

This is one of the more entertaining forms of syntax failure:

While decorating the house, a large spider dropped into the paint.

Now ruined by age and decay, I could still remember how the house had once looked.

Knocking apprehensively at the door of a shabby Victorian terraced house, an old man answered the door leaning heavily on his walking stick.

This is very similar to the 'dangling modifier', where the first part of the sentence isn't properly related to anything in the rest of it. Lots of inexperienced writers write sentences like the above, frequently with amusing results.

Here there's a problem with word order:

Two women who had retired for the night with their husbands and 30 sailors were missing, presumed drowned.

He remembered seeing a man who had looked just like Ronald at an evening of Shakespeare, who had stormed angrily into the bar during the interval.

I hope he got the Bard's autograph. Moving 'at an evening of Shakespeare' to the end would do the trick. Careful reading by the author should pick up errors like the above.

Unintended comedy

In which a part is taken to represent the whole (similar to synecdoche), but the effect is not as the author intended:

A man's heavy boots came rushing down the stairs.
She threw her head into his lap.
Suddenly he heard a car's engine go past.

It can be hard to spot this kind of thing in your own work, but again, you should try.

We need names

When you're writing a story, you know who is doing what and who is saying each line, because it's all in your head. The reader doesn't; you have to tell her. So be careful not to rely too much on pronouns:

The note stated that if she was the person she thought she was, she would be pleased to have her come to the house whenever she wished.

That sentence would probably be better recast, but if not, the author should let us know who is talking about whom by replacing some of those 'shes' with names.

The disembodied pronoun

He reached for his mobile, his hand shaking slightly as he tapped out the numbers. How long would he have to wait for the call to come?

That reads just fine – except that it's the very first paragraph and we have no idea yet who *he* is. It's bothering not to have a handle for somebody, so use their first name, surname or both right at the beginning. You can build up the character's identity and background progressively by feeding the reader references to his age, his physical type, his work, how he feels about life and so on as you go, either in the narrative or dialogue. Deal with the physical points early, as mentioned in the passage about creating characters in chapter 5, because the reader needs to be able to build a picture of your character in his mind's eye.

Me, myself and Irene

That harmless, necessary pronoun 'me' seems in some quarters to have become a pariah, a word to be skirted around. I frequently come across sentences like 'He invited Andrew and myself to the conference' and even 'Sophie and myself were invited'. Oh dear. Would you say 'He invited myself to the conference'? 'He invited Philip and I' is almost equally common. Perhaps there is something about the word 'me' which repels people, as if using it displayed some kind of self-obsession.

Are you a novelist or a scriptwriter?

Try not to take the idea of 'scenes' too far. It's clear from some manuscripts that the author is unconsciously writing not a novel but a film:

As he talked, the flames of the camp fire formed a blurred orange glow behind him.

Just then Dirk caught a reflection in Marianne's eyes – there was someone behind him! He whirled round just in time to knock the knife from Rodrigo's hand.

Philip got to his feet and took three paces towards the door. He half-opened it, looked both ways along the corridor, then turned back to Karl, who shook his head and turned away as if to leave. Philip took two paces back into the room and suddenly stopped, then slowly knelt down, putting his head in his hands.

You can see what's happened here. The writers have told their stories as if they were seeing them unfold on a cinema screen, and described the screenplay, right down to the out-of-focus camera. In the last two cases, we even get stage directions. A screenwriter has to use these devices, but you don't – in a novel you can describe the character's thoughts and feelings directly.

Narrative sequence

Most storytellers get their paragraphs in the right order. It's within sentences that things tend to go wrong. Each image, each idea, each action in the sentence has to be arranged correctly in relation to the others.

Jimmy increased his pace as the rain began to beat down.

But the rain came first, then the increase in pace – the above is not wrong, but it would be improved by changing it round:

As the rain began to beat down, Jimmy increased his pace.

She watched him read and re-read the letter, gasping in shock. He slumped into the chair.

The writer meant that the letter reader was gasping in shock. She should have written:

She watched him read and re-read the letter. He gasped in shock and slumped into the chair.

Harold came out of his reverie with a start as Gary switched on the music centre.

These events are related out of order; Harold woke up because of the sound from the music centre. It should be:

Gary switched on the music centre, and Harold came out of his reverie with a start.

Mary rushed inside, finding Matt lying in the corner.

So what did Mary do first – rush into the room or find Matt in the corner? It's not clear. This would have been better as:
Mary rushed inside to find Matt lying in the corner.

So when describing a sequence of events, make sure that everything that happened in each sentence is dealt with in the right order, or you'll cripple your narrative.

Of course there are times when you should relate events in the 'wrong' order, for example when you want to fill in a little background retrospectively in a few words:

Monty switched off the engine of the Morris, stretched his arms wide, yawned and pushed open the door. It had taken him two hours to drive to Marlborough and a twenty-minute traffic jam in the Malverns had left him in a foul mood.

This sentence is not ambiguous – it's just *flat*:

Kurt collapsed on the floor and Fred saw that he was holding a scrap of parchment in his yellowed fingers.

Much better as:

Kurt collapsed on the floor. That was when Fred saw that he was holding a scrap of parchment in his yellowed fingers.

And if we have already heard about the possible importance to the plot of a piece of parchment, this would be even better:

Kurt collapsed on the floor. That was when Fred saw that he was holding something in his yellowed fingers.
    A scrap of parchment.

Many writers instinctively start a sentence with its most

important part, yet this is often the least effective way of telling a story.

The painting had vanished the next day.
The next day, the painting had vanished.

In the first version, the vanishing is flatly reported, almost as if the painting in question had not been expected to hang around for long. In the second, there is an element of build-up, of suspense before the 'reveal'. Much better, and in the same number of words.

Number

The team was sweating with fatigue.
The couple is honeymooning in Barbados.
The audience was throwing bananas.
*A brood of 19 ducklings stays close to their mother (*a confused *Daily Telegraph* caption writer)

Strictly speaking collective nouns like these are indeed singular, but it gives me neckache to read sentences like the above. If treating 'family' and 'team' as if they were plural ideas is illegal, the law is an ass.

Borrowing from other writers

Contrary to the assumption of many, you don't need to ask before quoting from published work, as long as you don't use too much of it. If you have used material from other people's writings you are expected to acknowledge it by naming the source publication and the author, particularly in professional and technical books. It is the convention in publishing that you may quote 400 words from copyrighted text in a single extract without seeking permission, or 800 words in total.

CHAPTER 13

Style, language, grammar and other matters

By now I know some readers will be saying, 'Stop giving me rules, I'm a writer! My creativity must not be stifled!' That's fine, as long as you remember that our system of grammar and syntax is not there to make life difficult but to aid meaning. If you break the rules carelessly, your readers simply won't understand what you're trying to tell them. Accomplished writers consciously break rules and get away with it, but first you must know what those rules are.

A word about syntax

Syntax (which literally means 'arranging together') is a broad term which refers to the relationships between words and phrases in a sentence. Over and above grammar, spelling and punctuation, syntax faults are the most widespread errors of new authors, and the considerable challenges of English syntax in particular appear to be the biggest headache for non-native speakers. In some books I have edited there are syntax faults in almost every sentence, although grammar and spelling may be largely correct.

Native English writers tend to produce sentences which pretty much make sense but are spoiled by clumsy syntax:

When I saw what some of the girls wore in class I often thought how bad their appearance had to be before they were excluded.

They amused the onlookers by one grabbing the ball and racing round their enclosure, while the others gave chase.

Whereas non-native writers tend to use the right words in the wrong relationships:

Even the road did not have a bridge to go across.

The rain suddenly fell more heavy, it was getting darker like night now and time to Foo Shen for going in her home.

Spelling

Yes, use a spellchecker; no, don't trust it. And try not to forget which side of the Atlantic you live on. British authors should be aware of American spellings, and vice versa. We are exposed to so much American material that it's easy to get confused. In a sense it doesn't really matter, but I do think you should at least recognise which spelling belongs on which continent, so that you can be consistent. I recently had an edited MS returned to me with all the spellings mysteriously Americanised. On this occasion the author was British and wanted English spellings, but his spellchecker, annoyingly for both of us, had disobeyed him and he hadn't noticed, so we had to clear up the mess. See Appendix III for a collection of English v. American spellings.

Here are some of the most popular misspellings in the books I edit. Many of them are clearly down to simple confusion between two very similar words.

lead (for led, the past tense of to lead)
lightening (lightning)
draw (for drawer)
loose (for lose)
definately (definitely)
publically (publicly)
momento (memento)
pharoah (pharaoh)
reign (for rein)
ecstacy (ecstasy)
peddle (for pedal)
slither (for sliver)
horde (for hoard)
prize (for prise)

The second week of October will likely be remembered as the moment when the 2016 presidential campaign went careening off the rails and spinning into the void. – BBC News website

A few words are confused so frequently that I fear it is inevitable we will lose one of them. The word 'careened', for example, has long meant to turn over a boat in order to clean it. More and more often I see it used in placed of 'careered', as above. The use of 'sat' in place of 'seated' and 'stood' in place of 'standing' is so common I can see it being accepted as correct before long ('he was sat' means someone sat him).

Lay and lie

I just wanted to lay down and die.

Millions of people in the UK now use the verb 'lay' (present tense) where 'lie' is correct. I wouldn't mind so much, but 'lay' has its own, distinct meaning, like 'career'. It's a transitive verb, so it has to have an object – 'I helped to lay the foundations'.

May and might

If I had a sheet of A4 paper for every time I've seen an author wrongly use 'may' instead of 'might', I would never need to go the stationer's. Here is an example from a source that should know better, the BBC news website again:

Former News of the World editor Andy Coulson has said he may not have become David Cameron's communications director if he had revealed his knowledge of phone-hacking.

'May' is used when it's possible that the event described actually happened, but we don't know either way. 'Might' is used when it could have happened, but we know it didn't.

Tenses

Confusion between tenses is very common among amateur authors – particularly the pluperfect. This is the 'double past', the tense to use when the event described was in the past at the time of description, eg 'he had told him not to do it'. Using the wrong tense isn't just a technical detail, it can confuse the meaning and may have the reader (and the editor) scratching their heads.

I took Alexander to London, where he grew up.
Presumably you bought him a junior ticket for the outward journey and an adult one for the return.

When I see the present tense crop up in a narrative, I know there's going to be trouble ahead, because authors hardly ever manage to use it consistently. It's common in conversation to switch to the present when giving a blow-by-blow account of an event – 'this bloke comes up to me and says…' You can do this in writing too, notably to deal with particularly intense passages describing feelings. But it needs to be carefully controlled, and any one passage needs to be consistently in one tense or the other, or the reader will become very confused about what is happening now and what happened some time ago. Some authors set out to write a whole book in the present tense, but soon discover how difficult it is to write narrative text without resorting to the past tense. It can be done, with care, but it's probably safest to avoid it except for passages where you are describing a particular scene and want to use the extra impact the present tense can give you, or if you are describing an imagined scene, or a dream.

Italics and inverted commas (quote marks)

It is customary (though by no means compulsory) to use italics on the titles of creative works, ie books, plays and films, and on the names of ships. They are not used on the names of pubs, clubs, companies, brand names etc. If for some reason a whole passage is in italics, for example if it's a footnote, any book titles and the like within it should appear in roman (non-italic) text.

Italics can also be used for emphasis where the word emphasised is not obvious from the context, eg 'at least she is not wearing a *green* silk dress'. In business writing underlining or bold are normally used for emphasis, but when you're reading a book, this feels a bit like being punched in the eye; italics are far more elegant.

Words and phrases from a foreign language are traditionally italicised, at least on the first occasion, unless they have been adopted into English, like 'au pair' and 'kindergarten'.

Inverted commas (quotation marks) are not used on the names of people or places, though they may serve as a substitute for italics on book titles etc as above. They are used when the reference is to the word itself rather than the person or thing it stands for, eg 'Did you know 'syzygy' is the only English word with three Ys in it?'

The misextended list

Lots of people write this sort of thing:

She was wearing a green dress, a pair of black shoes and smiled at me.

They sat quietly in the corner of the restaurant, ordered two brandies and Jimmy explained his dilemma to Ricardo.

Easily fixed with a bit of punctuation:

They sat quietly in the corner of the restaurant and ordered two brandies while Jimmy explained his dilemma to Ricardo.

More popular mistakes

The **passive voice** is best avoided in most cases. It is much better to say 'we decided to build a new factory' than 'it was decided to build a new factory'.

Sentence structure defeats more people than you would believe. Sentences can fail for dozens of reasons, most of which I hope are covered in this book. Sentences can be as long or as short as you like, as long as they are assembled correctly – sentences that lose their way are a terrible obstacle to the reader. Fragments (verbless sentences, in effect) are fine, as long as they are short and deliberate. It's OK to begin a sentence with 'and' or 'but'. It is not OK to have two buts in a sentence.

Numbers – there is no hard and fast rule, but with larger numbers and precise quantities most publishers favour numerals, while with shorter numbers and those used in a more general sense we prefer letters, so we would write 'our profit increased from 4% to 11%' but 'he kept over a hundred sheep'.

Brackets – stick to standard curved brackets. The square bracket is reserved for use when you need brackets within brackets, or when something has been inserted by the author to add information within a quotation, for example 'Every time

I read *Pride and Prejudice* I want to dig [Jane Austen] up and beat her over the skull with her own shin-bone.' (Mark Twain, by the way – I wonder why he kept re-reading it?)

Wage war on gratuitous **capital letters**. Capitalitis is a national disease to which few people are immune, and many of the manuscripts we receive are full of nouns with unnecessary initial caps, usually on the words the writer feels are important – director, doctor, solicitor, company, centre, university. No noun needs a capital unless it is part of a title or name ('the church was called the Parish Church of St Stephen'). Even admirals and archbishops get lower case, unless you are referring to a specific holder of the rank. And so do gods, in general, though a capital is correct when you are talking about God by name.

The same rule applies to mother, father, granddad and so on; they all take lower case when used as ordinary nouns ('his mother told him'… but capitals when used as names ('Good morning, Mother').

Incidentally you should not use a capital on a 'the' preceding a proper name, unless it is specifically part of the title – *The Times*, but not The Falkland Islands or The Dog and Duck. There's been a proliferation of this in recent years, perhaps caused by our constant exposure to logos, signs, advertising etc in which 'The' is capitalised, but it is not standard English and looks, I think, rather ridiculous.

Lots of people, having seen 'sir' and 'madam' correctly capitalised many times as part of a title, wrongly capitalise them when used as salutations.

North, south, east and west don't take capitals either, except as part of the name of a recognised place, like East Africa or South America.

Avoid **collective direct speech**. It's surprising how often people write such statements as 'They said, 'we're going to the pub later, why don't you join us?'' People never speak with one voice, unless they are taking part in a church service or a military drill, so the speaker should always be an individual.

CHAPTER 14

Punctuation for authors

This is a subject in its own right and you're advised to get a book (or three) on it unless you are very sure of your skill with the language, but here are some basics, arising from my own experience in editing manuscripts.

The full stop

Many amateur authors seem to share the same problem with the full stop – they don't use it anywhere near enough. Many, many writers fail to recognise when a sentence has died on its feet and it's time to put it out of its misery and start a new one. Long sentences often read much better split into two or three.

He was responding well to the medication and if only he had been calmer and had not kept refusing to eat he would have had a chance of recovery, but you could not blame him, he did not understand that she was dying.

There are too many ideas chasing each other in that clumsy, rushed sentence. How much better it would read split into several sentences:

He was responding well to the medication. If only he had been calmer and had not kept refusing to eat, he would have had a chance of recovery. Yet you could not blame him; he did not understand that he was dying.

Sometimes the fault lies in the clumsy repetition of 'that' or 'which'. Here again, wonders can be achieved with the full stop:

We had been given a sweet little Yorkshire terrier which we called Rags, which the children adored and which gave us much pleasure but which Colin and I had to walk most of the time.

Much better as:

We had been given a sweet little Yorkshire terrier which we called Rags. The children adored him and he gave us much pleasure, but Colin and I had to walk him most of the time.

An introduction to the comma

The harmless little **comma** seems to cause more trouble than any other punctuation mark. You ought to know how to use commas, because they can be critical to meaning (consider the difference between 'he stopped waiting for me' and 'he stopped, waiting for me').

In fact the comma has half a dozen separately-defined functions, and you should never use one just because it seems a long time since you last stuck in some punctuation. To understand all the subtleties of comma use, you'll need to consult a grammar guide, but here is a practical summary for authors.

The one thing everybody seems to know about the comma is that you mustn't use it before 'and' or 'but'. In fact it's probably the one rule that isn't true. Sentences are often hobbled by slavish adherence to this rule. The following are perfectly correct:

Yes, and he told me he was leaving.

Lucy thought I should stay in London, and perhaps she was right.

Here deleting the comma would change the meaning:

She was annoyed when I wanted to fry some bacon, and refused to do the washing up.

The Gnostic Christians were persecuted after Rome converted to Christianity, and most of the texts were burned.

Similarly:

The MP Hugh Ross said...
The MP, Hugh Ross, said...

In the first, Hugh Ross (the subject of the sentence) is being described as an MP; in the second 'The MP' is the subject of the sentence, and the phrase between commas identifies him as Hugh Ross.

I went with my friend Mark and his wife
- Mark is a friend.
I went with my friend, Mark, and his wife
- I have only one friend, and his name is Mark.

You can work these out for yourself:

When are we going to attack, Mike?
Stop, dancing woman!
What is this thing called, love?

The train stopped only once in London
The train stopped only once, in London

Why is it a problem?
Why, is it a problem?

Abigail too was excited to have landed a job, with the World Health Organisation.

Deleting the comma after 'job' would mean Abigail's job was also with the WHO.

I went to see a colleague, Joan Smith, who had been at Oxford with me and read the riot act.

A comma after 'me' would change the subject of 'read' from Joan to the speaker.

His favourite trick was to wear a gorilla suit, purchased from a joke shop whenever a senior official was visiting the yard.

You need a comma after 'shop', otherwise the speaker is saying he bought a new gorilla suit every time the official came.

Sometimes the only solution is a change in word order:

We were met by an officer wearing civilian clothes from the British Embassy.

The comma is largely used to avoid ambiguity, and this use generally overrides other considerations. Here are some examples.

Dr Smith, the stationmaster, and a person of some consequence in the village.

We could be talking about three people here. Ditch the second comma.

Sometimes lots of commas are needed:

He picked it up, then, satisfied, passed it to Desmond, his assistant, who was at his side.

Commas in lists

Commas are useful when a sentence consist of two longish independent clauses:
I have long been a fan of Mozart, and I have a large collection of his music.

And after initial adverbs:
However, I was prepared to make an exception.

To indicate omission and avoid consequent ambiguity:
My first wife was French; the second, German.

When addressing someone:
It is my view, Mr President, that this country has no place in such a conflict.

After quoted words, eg:
My father told me 'You are an idiot', something I have never forgotten.

(In American English it's usual to put that comma above inside the quotation mark.)

Where commas should not be used

Just because it's a long time since you used one and need to take a breath:
The very considerable interval since the last health and safety assessment had been carried out, necessitated a full

reappraisal of our factory procedures to be made to the next board meeting.

So do really short sentences ever need commas? Sometimes, yes.

A comma is never used between a subject and a verb.

Commas between adjectives

A distant, hot star (a star which is both hot and distant)
A distant neutron star (a neutron star which is distant)
A loud, continuous, mournful whining (a whining which is three quite distinct things: loud, continuous and mournful)

The comma is used where the adjectives are 'coordinate', ie they could be reversed – in other words they each act separately on the noun; it's not appropriate if the words would sound odd reversed, eg *a black small dog.*

The closer the association between the second adjective and the noun, the weaker the case for the comma. This is because the second adjective and noun are bundled together in our minds as if they formed a noun. There is no precise dividing line between the two kinds, of course. It's largely a matter of instinct and experience.

Colons, semi-colons and dashes

As Lynne Truss points out in her entertaining book *Eats, Shoots & Leaves*, the often-abused colon and semi-colon are all about expectation; they 'propel you forward in a sentence towards more information'. I think that is a clearer way of looking at them than any other definition I've seen.

Semi-colon use has declined over the years, like the wearing of hats, but some authors (dare I say older authors?) still use them in almost every sentence, which can become very irksome, like a speech affectation.

It's very common for authors to use semi-colons as if they were just 'strong' commas, probably because they imagine that punctuation has something to do with length of pause, which it hasn't, except in one respect; adding punctuation does slow text down. Just as some people speak fast, some authors write fast, omitting commas, in particular, where most of us might feel they are needed. I don't think that's a bad thing – it conveys a sense of pace, like the instruction '*allegro*' or '*vivace*' in musical notation.

In fact the semi-colon's job is quite different from that of the comma. The words after it should form an independent clause, ie they should stand by themselves as a sentence – in other words, they need their own verb. If you can't replace the semi-colon with a full stop to create two grammatical sentences, it may be you should have used a comma.

The colon is more heavy-duty than its gentler brother; it works as an announcement of information to come, saying, in effect, 'and the winners are:' or 'and the reason is as follows:' Incidentally it is quite common in American usage to put a capital after a colon, but this is not correct in British English.

The dash is very similar in function to the comma, but has more – well, dash. Its energy and sense of speed have long made it cherished by newspaper sub-editors (I fell in love with it myself at first sight, when I discovered its value as a young reporter). It is best used when applied in pairs for a snappy aside: 'Though we had very little money – father was earning only £20 a week – we all had new toys at Christmas'. Many authors who have discovered it tend to use it too much. It should not be used as if it was a comma: 'He opened the door – told her to get in – and drove off'.

The exclamation mark

Use one only after what grammarians call ejaculations ('Crikey!') and short, sudden statements such as 'He's behind you!', not in an attempt to show that a statement is odd or amusing. An exclamation mark after a funny line is the equivalent of laughing at your own joke. The words should create the exclamation mark in the reader's mind; don't use one to hammer them in.

The question mark

These should be used on questions, obviously, but only direct questions, never on indirect questions, although many, many people do this:

What are you doing tomorrow? (right)
He asked me what I was doing tomorrow? (wrong)

It is common practice, and perfectly acceptable, to use a question mark on a statement to indicate that it is intended as a question:

You're looking for Mr Prendergast?

Put your question marks in the right place. I see this a lot:

Why don't you join us, there's plenty to go round?

It should of course be:
Why don't you join us? There's plenty to go round.

The apostrophe

I trod on a wasp's nest.
Poor little creature.

Putting an apostrophe before the 's' when it should be after, or vice versa, or using one where it doesn't belong at all, is confusing and sometimes amusing. By far the commonest mistake with the apostrophe is to mix up singular and plural (as above). It's easy to be caught out by words which pluralise without an 's', like 'children' – possessive form 'children's'.

Plurals, by the way, do not have apostrophes, including those of numbers and abbreviations – 1970s, MPs.

The hyphen

Hyphens are used to avoid ambiguity, often with good reason:

Extra marital sex
Twenty odd vicars

Some compound nouns are usually hyphenated, some are usually unhyphenated (so they are not really compound nouns any more) and some are usually run together; which is correct is very often a matter of taste. Paintbrush, stagecoach and mothball are surely written thus, but what about fairy tale, watchtower, coffee pot, tablecloth, fishing-rod, soulmate, roadworks, doorbell, wasteland, head-dress, pony tail and stair carpet? No two people will come up with exactly the same answers.

Hyphens may also be used to avoid 'letter collision', when the lack of a hyphen would make the word look odd, eg in re-entry and un-American. But you don't need one in most 're' or 'un' words, like rejoin or undeveloped.

And another thing…

The trail of dots… (properly known as the ellipsis) is written as three dots with no space in front. It is used to indicate an unfinished statement and is not a substitute for a comma, semicolon etc.

It's considered unnecessary these days to use full points after initials – it's better to write A J Smith and USA. It's no longer customary to use full points after Mr, Mrs and Dr, either.

CHAPTER 15

Prefaces, forewords, acknowledgements, dedications and other bolt-on accessories

At the beginning of the book:

You may wish to include a **dedication**, which will usually say something like 'To Mary, without whom this book could never have been written'. You don't need to head it 'dedication', as that's obvious from the wording.

The **contents** (not 'table of contents', far too formal) lists the material in the book, with page numbers. One is required in most books, but you do not need one if the chapters are numbered but untitled, as in many works of fiction. Traditionally, contents lists often used to include a summary of the contents of each chapter (I start work – my first court case – moving to London, etc) and some older authors still favour this practice.

The **foreword** (optional) is traditionally written by someone other than the author at their invitation, and acts as an introduction and endorsement of the book. It is most definitely not spelt 'forward', as a surprising number of people seem to think. If you know someone who is well-known and has some connection to yourself and the subject of the book, invite them to do your foreword. But be cautious; foreword writers have a habit of submitting something quite different from what you had in mind, so it's wise to give some guidance.

A **preface** (optional) may be added to explain how or why the book was written.

A **prologue** (optional) is designed to set the scene for the book by telling an earlier story which is linked to it, or by bringing forward a key episode from the book itself, to draw the reader in early (see Chapter 5).

Acknowledgements are the author's thanks to people who have helped in some way, by providing information or giving permissions. They should be kept reasonably succinct; gushing praise looks amateurish, and makes it harder to be even-handed.

Credits should be given to anyone who has provided permission to use pictures, quoted material etc, eg 'The picture on page 17 has been used by kind permission of…'

You may want to include a **disclaimer** if you are concerned that you may, for example, have used a picture without permission because you could not trace the copyright owner, or to make it clear that fictitious characters are not intended to refer to actual people. The precise wording is not critical, but I suggest something like this: 'The author and publisher have made every effort to contact holders of copyright relating to material used in this book. If it appears that any item has been reproduced without permission, they will be pleased to make the necessary arrangements'.

The **introduction** (useful in a factual book) is a summary of what the book is about and what it is intended to achieve. It is usually the last item before chapter 1.

At the end of a factual book:

An **epilogue** is sometimes included to sum up the book and 'sign off'.

A **postscript** may be written to bring the reader up to date on events since the book was written or to add supplementary information.

Appendices are the place to put reference material such as lists, tables of data and reports referred to in the text.

A **glossary** may be included if specialist or technical language or foreign or slang words have been used extensively.

A **bibliography** points the reader to further reading on the subject or related matters, and/or to sources used by the author; important in academic or technical works. List the title, author, year and publisher, but you don't need to bother with the ISBN, or to give page references, unless you really want to.

An **index** is included in a factual book where the author wants readers to be able to find references to particular people, organisations or events. Compiling an index is an exacting and time-consuming task, and it's best done by the author. There is nothing automatic about the process, as judgments have to be made about which terms and which occurrences of those terms are to be included. By no means should you index all names, places etc in your book, only those which people may want to look up, and not passing references ('after visiting Marianne we continued south via Paris'), only informative ones

(Marianne was on excellent form/we spent an enjoyable weekend in Paris).

A properly-structured index requires the (expensive) services of a professional indexer, but it's easy enough for an author to compile a simple one. Don't waste time entering the index page numbers on your manuscript, because by the time is book is typeset they will be completely different. At the artwork stage you will probably be dealing with PDF (Adobe Acrobat) files. You will need to use the word search facility in Acrobat to find each occurrence of each indexed term, decide whether it's worth including, and list the folio (printed page) number. This cannot be done until the book's artwork is final – jump the gun and you may have to do it all over again, because adding or subtracting material could change all the page numbers that follow.

An index can easily turn into a can of worms for both the author and the typographer, so if you do need an index we suggest you keep it simple.

Covers and flaps

The back cover of a paperback usually carries a brief description of the book, designed to summarise its contents and pique the interest of readers. No text is printed on the inside of a paperback cover. Hardbacks may be supplied with a separate dust jacket, in which case a few lines of additional text are usually prepared to appear upon it – additional description of the book, an author profile or an extract from the text, chosen to help 'sell' the book to the potential purchaser.

PART THREE

PUBLISHING

CHAPTER 16

Preparing and presenting your manuscript

You've spent months, perhaps years, working on your book, and finally it's beginning to look as if it's ready for publication. In fact almost every manuscript requires some attention from an editor before it is in good enough shape to publish. Even the best submissions contain minor errors of spelling, punctuation or syntax, while many manuscripts need partial rewriting to make them read well. All authors, however good their command of English, make mistakes.

Some authors claim to have edited their own books. Certainly you should check and revise your MS over and over until it's as good as you can get it, but most people make the same habitual mistakes in English and you will inevitably be blind to yours, or you wouldn't be making them in the first place. It's also unlikely, however talented a writer you are, that you will have as good or correct a command of English as a professional editor. That's why even the world's finest authors all work with editors.

This doesn't mean you shouldn't check and check again before submitting your MS, particularly matters of fact, like names and dates. No book should be published until the manuscript has been carefully checked and corrected, and no reputable publisher will agree to put out an uncorrected book, because it will reflect badly on them. Astonishingly enough, some of the biggest self-publishing companies do appear to publish books without even a rudimentary edit. Some of them are full of mistakes, and there are real car crashes out there. We've seen books for sale on the internet which were packed with syntactical and grammatical howlers. Inspection reveals that they have been spell-checked, but have clearly been nowhere near an editor.

Authors in this position are usually horrified when they're told what a poor state their books are in. 'But Megabucks Publishing would have sorted all that out, wouldn't they?' they plead. No they wouldn't, not if the author agreed to go ahead without paying a separate editing fee.

The fact is, if you wish to offer your book for sale, it will almost certainly need professional editing to ensure it does not disappoint the people who are going to buy it – and not just to correct the text. Someone who knows what they're doing also needs to make sure that the story makes sense, with the right events dealt with in the right order. The people and places in the story need to be properly introduced and described. The author often fails to notice that he has not explained who Roberto is (or has done so twice), or that he has forgotten to tell us where he lives (if that's important). This is because the story, along with all the characters and locations, is already in the author's head. The editor has never encountered Roberto before, so she notices such problems immediately.

A good editor will be happy to sort all these issues out for you and turn your rough draft into a polished book, in collaboration with you, but it will save you time and money if your MS is in reasonably good shape before you submit it.

Getting a second opinion

It may be helpful to show your manuscript to someone else – a friend or relative who's hot on grammar and spelling, for example, or has an understanding of the subject matter. If you do this, I suggest you don't introduce it by saying 'Here's my new book, I'm so proud of it, what do you think?' This will give your friend little choice but to agree that it's wonderful. Instead say, 'Here's my book, I'm still working on it. Any ideas for what I could do to improve it?' That way you're likely to get a much more valuable response.

Please make sure that if you're going to run your MS past a friend, you do so BEFORE submitting it to your publisher. If well-meaning friends try to put their stamp on the book after it's been professionally edited, you'll be faced with the choice of ignoring their advice or going back to the editor to make a further round of changes, which will have to be paid for and may well be challenged. More than once we have received a set of erroneous 'corrections' from a friend or relative of the author after editing and have had to explain why we would not be implementing most of them. One woman sent in her autobiography, saying her daughter, a PhD graduate, had edited and checked it, and accordingly our editing services would not be required. The MS was stuffed with basic errors, and as she was unwilling to pay us to put them right, we had to decline the book.

If you do decide to show your book to someone else after it has been edited or even typeset, please make it clear that you do not want to them make creative changes or to add or subtract material – just to scan the text for errors. It's useful if they pick up subtle slips of the word processor which have been missed, but I can't tell you how irritating it is to be sent a list of misguided grammatical or spelling 'corrections' from someone who seems to assume that their knowledge of English outranks that of a professional editor. Favourites that come to mind include changing 'of John and me' back to 'of John and I', moving commas or quotation marks to the wrong positions and putting capitals back on to all kinds of 'important' words like 'royal' and 'university' which do not take them unless used as part of a title (see page 174).

Presentation

Keep your manuscript plain and simple. Many authors set out their text using elaborate fonts and flourishes, fiddling with spacing and indents and leading (the space between lines), even perhaps changing the page area from the standard A4 to A5, or one of the standard book sizes, all in an effort to make their work look more like a book. However at this stage it is not a book, and a number of things have to be done to it before it becomes one. Fussy formatting, fancy fonts and funny furbelows will just make you look like an amateur. In any case the editor will remove your formatting with a few cruel keystrokes, so that she has a plain MS to work on. She knows that the designer will design and format the text professionally later.

Your book should be written in Word, with minimal formatting other than paragraph indents and page numbers. Courier is a standard industry typeface for manuscripts, but any clear font, such as Verdana, Calibri or Helvetica, will do fine. Times New Roman is still very popular, though it's not my favourite, because the very fine punctuation marks can be hard to check. Comic Sans is the primary school teachers' font – soft, friendly and easy to read, but a trifle patronising for anyone over the age of eleven. Stick to one plain font throughout, unless you specifically want to indicate that certain passages, quotations for example, should stand out when typeset. A typographer will know how to do this properly, but you can help by, for example, setting main headings all in the same font/weight and any subheadings in a different font/weight, so the editor knows immediately which is which. If you like to use italics for quoted verse, for example, by all means pass this preference on to the typographer. One of the advantages of self-publishing is that you do get some say about such matters – though you will be (or should be) advised if your requirements won't work on the page. You will get a very old-fashioned look from a trade publisher if you start querying their typography.

You may find it easier to write the chapters as separate computer files, but once it's ready to be submitted it's better to present your MS on a single file, including all the chapters, the title, the foreword and so on. This ensures the material is all present and correct and in the right order. It also makes reviewing and editing much easier. When I am sent a manuscript as a number of files, the first thing I do is to join them all together. When I come across an error which is repeated through the MS, such as a consistently-misspelt word or the insertion of erroneous gaps in front of punctuation marks, I can use search and replace in Word to correct them all in one go. Having the book in one file also makes it much easier to check for unwarranted repetition and ensure events are told in the right order.

Always work on an A4 page size, regardless of the eventual format of the book, and set generous margins top, bottom and sides, and wide line spacing (around 1.5-2). This is standard industry practice and makes it much easier for marks to be written up on a printout if necessary. In the days before computers, keeping to the same font size, type area and spacing enabled editors (of both newspapers and books) to assess word count quickly; these days the computer will do that for you regardless of formatting, so it's less critical, but it is still a good discipline to follow.

Text should be ranged left ('ragged right'), not justified both sides, at the editing stage – it is easier both to read and to edit. It will usually be set justified both sides when it is typeset for the book.

If you're including any quotations from printed works, short ones of a line or two can be included in the paragraph in quotes or italics, while longer ones should be given paragraphs of their own and set in italics or indented. However the actual setting will usually be determined by the typographer when your book is put together.

Boxes, tables, diagrams, graphic devices, indents, columns, bulleted lists etc should be used with care. The fiddlier your formatting, the greater the chance of your carefully-laid-out text turning to hieroglyphics as soon as the document is reformatted. For this reason, with anything but the simplest tables, it's best to prepare the graphics as separate documents, numbered in sequence and with corresponding numbers inserted in the text – 'INSERT GRAPHIC 7'.

Do not include images in your word document; doing so usually reduces the definition and will make the file large and unwieldy. In any case they will probably be stripped out before editing. Send them separately, as a set of individual numbered files, with an accompanying and matching list of captions. If I'm sent a 50-megabyte MS with a collection of fancy fonts and variable setting, studded with images and graphics, I copy the whole document into Microsoft Notepad, then cut and paste it back into Word before I start work. Very satisfying, like stripping wallpaper. Of course I keep the original for reference.

Remember that the page numbers on the manuscript will not match those in the final typeset text – they are just a working reference, so there's no point in putting page numbers in the contents. Nor will the page turns match those in the printed book, so you shouldn't worry if, for example, a heading falls at the bottom of a page; the typographer will make sure that doesn't happen in the book.

One of the first operations I perform on a new MS is to use the search and replace function to delete all the double character spaces. This is partly because we follow the usual industry standard of putting just one space between sentences. The other reason is that many authors use the space bar somewhat recklessly to create space where they want it, eg for indenting (which should be done in the 'paragraph' menu in Word).

If you insert page numbers, make sure you use the page numbering option in Word, so they appear in the page header or footer – on no account write them at the top or bottom of the text area, because every time changes to the manuscript alter the page turns, all the page numbers that follow will disappear into the text. If the editor has also globally deleted all your double spaces as above, you will get sentences like 'What are you 127 talking about, you silly man?' Imagine trying to weed out all the stray page numbers from 1-400 from the lines they are buried in, particularly in an MS which happens to contain a lot of numbers which do belong there.

Pictures and other illustrations

Factual books are usually improved by the inclusion of pictures, whether they are photographs old or new, paintings, drawings, diagrams or old documents. Illustrations add to the interest and impact of the book, but they also add to the printing cost, particularly if you want them in colour, so it's best to be selective.

If you're taking photos for your book, shoot them at high resolution on a proper camera - although I must admit that today's mobile phones can produce astonishing results in good light, if used with care. Don't overestimate your own abilities as a photographer – amateurish shots will make the whole book look amateurish. Old photos, eg family snapshots, are fine, and almost anything can be reproduced, however grainy and murky it is, as long as you don't expect it to look any clearer on the printed page than it does in your father's photo album. However your book will look better if you're choosy with your pictures, and if you're hoping for sales you should try to be as selective as possible.

Scrapbook items such as old newspaper cuttings, letters, passports, Forces documents and so on are best reproduced as they are, complete with frayed and curling edges. If you try to crop the image you will usually spoil it, not least because they are rarely exactly square. Either photograph them (flat on a plain background) or get them scanned, or pass them to the publisher to scan them (after extracting a promise that they will be returned safely to you).

As mentioned, graphics, tables, diagrams and so on should be supplied as separate files. If you're preparing your own, make sure the publisher can use them before you do too much work.

Authors sometimes forget that a book page is a lot smaller than many documents, and there's a limit to what you can fit onto it. When a large drawing or graphic is reduced to fit your book, fine detail may disappear or become illegible. Detailed maps, family trees etc may not be reproducible at the size of a book page – they may need to be simplified, retouched or divided into two or more separate images.

It's best to supply images as separate JPEG files, clearly numbered for reference, with captions included in the main text (if they are to be used with the text) or on a separate file cross-referenced to the numbers. Do not compile pictures on a Word document, PDF or Publisher file, except possibly for separate reference.

If the image has been created by someone else, they will automatically own the copyright. Your publisher will advise you, but you should do what you can to obtain permission for all third-party illustrations to be used in your book, including those downloaded from the internet. It's accepted, however, that it may not be possible to trace the artist or photographer after a number of years, so if you're including material of unknown origin, or which was taken or created by someone you can't contact, you may wish to include a disclaimer along the lines of *'Every effort has been made to trace copyright holders. If you are concerned that any image in this book has been used without permission, please contact the publisher'*.

Usually pictures will be printed in sets of glossy pages, generally one or two, depending on the number there are. If you want your pictures to be embedded in the text at certain points, you will need to specify this. Don't expect them to appear exactly beside the sentence they refer to, as the typographer has to allow for page breaks. Books with embedded pictures will usually cost more to edit, design and print, particularly if the pictures are in colour, because coated paper will have to be used throughout. Amazon, incidentally, tend to put much higher prices on books with colour photos.

Copyrighting your book

Some authors fret obsessively about protecting their copyright, typing a little '©Angela Anxious' on every page and imagining that their work could be stolen from them and used by some dastardly person to make money. One prospective client even insisted on travelling to the office to show us her book, then taking it away again, in case we fiendish fellows at Mereo took the opportunity to copy it while her back was turned and sell it under our own name. The truth is that very few manuscripts have any value to anyone except the author. If your book is the lost war diary of Field Marshal Montgomery or an undiscovered novel by Virginia Woolf, it's obviously a special case and needs to be protected. If it's all your own work, whether a memoir, a novel or a book of poetry, it is very unlikely to have any value to anyone but yourself.

We have worked with one author who apparently did have her book, or rather the ideas behind it, stolen, by a trusted employee who passed it on to a successful writer, who then apparently used the material as the basis for a novel; she has spent half her life trying to prove plagiarism, so far unsuccessfully. This, however, is extremely rare.

Having said all this, it is so easy to protect your copyright that you would be silly not to do so. Copyright exists automatically in any original work; all you have to do is make sure you can prove you wrote your book first, just in case anyone ever tries to pass it off as their own. There are firms out there that will take your money for the privilege of registering copyright, but this is quite unnecessary. All you need do is share the document with a reliable third party – your publisher, a trusted friend, your solicitor – anyone who will acknowledge receipt and possession of a copy of the file on a certain date and promise to keep the file or document in case it's ever needed as evidence. You will then be able to sleep at night, knowing that in the highly unlikely event of someone 'borrowing' your work you'll be able to prove in perpetuity that you wrote it first. This won't necessarily stop people from copying your stuff or adapting it to their own ends, but if you find out, you'll have a chance of doing something about it.

Sending in your MS

Finally, when you are ready to send your manuscript to a publisher, here are a few ground rules.

1   Read the instructions – send what the publisher has asked for, in the format they stipulate.

2   While conventional publishers still tend to expect submissions in hard copy, electronic submissions are safer and far more convenient. Paper manuscripts are clumsy, unnecessary and expensive to post (and have a habit of getting lost). An editor can't do anything with a paper manuscript anyway, until it's been scanned to create a digital file, and scanning invariably creates typographical errors (an 'l' reads as a '1' or or an 'rn' reads as an 'm'). If you do have to send paper, always keep a copy, in case it's lost. You'd be amazed how many people send in their only copy.

3   Email is king. The easiest and most efficient and secure way to send your MS is simply to send the text in a single file as an email attachment to a short introductory message. A lot of authors seem to feel email somehow isn't serious enough for something as important as a manuscript – not so. You could also send it on a memory stick or CD if you prefer, but there is no advantage in doing this.

4   Don't put a copyright notice on your MS (as mentioned, copyright exists automatically) but do put your name and contact details on the first page and your initials or surname, plus the title of the book (or a short form of it), on every page, in the header.

5   Do include a covering letter which explains what your book is about and who you are. Don't 'sell' the book as if you were writing a mailshot for a commercial product – it must sell itself.

6   Don't send photos (if any) with an initial submission. When you are invited to send them, package them properly and

label them, then use the Royal Mail's special delivery or a courier, not ordinary post.

7   Be very careful about mass emailing the same submission to a list of publishers, particularly trade publishers. You have a better chance of being taken seriously if you approach them one at a time. A publisher is less likely to engage with you and give your submission serious consideration if they know you've sent the same proposal to a long list of people.

8   If you want the MS back, particularly if it's unsolicited, enclose a suitable stamped addressed envelope.

CHAPTER 17

The world of publishing

There are many ways of publishing a book these days, but most of them can be categorised as either conventional publishing, where the publisher pays, and self-publishing, where the author pays. It's a bit more complicated than that, however, as I will explain.

Conventional (trade) publishing

'It has been well said that an author who expects results from a first novel is in a position similar to that of a man who drops a rose petal down the Grand Canyon of Arizona and listens for the echo.' – P G Wodehouse

Put simply, conventional or trade publishers pay authors for their books, invest money in editing, designing, printing and publicising them, then sell as many copies as they can at as high a price as possible and give the author a small percentage of the profits (if any) back as royalties. They will usually offer an advance, to lock the author into a contract. For authors who haven't yet established a reputation this is likely to be no more than a few thousand pounds at the very most, but the big publishers occasionally offer huge sums, if they think they are on to something big and are planning to invest in marketing it; the amount is based on how many books they think the author can sell, and is often based on a deal for two or more titles.

The advance is usually paid in stages, say 50% on submission of manuscript and 50% on publication. The royalty rate usually varies depending on the format and the sales channel – typically somewhere between 8-15%. No royalties are paid until the book has earned its advance. It's reputed, though hard to prove, that 70% of books fail to do that, so don't count on earning any money from your book on top of the advance.

A trade publisher may invest anything from a few thousand to £50,000 or more in your book, depending on the likely rewards. Every book they take on is a risk; the idea is that a few big hits will pay for the many flops. Where famous names are concerned the risk to publishers can be massive, and they come unstuck all the time. Pippa Middleton's book *Celebrate* earned her a £400,000 advance, but sold only 18,000 copies. Arnold Schwarzenegger's autobiography *Total Recall* sold 27,000 copies in the first month, which doesn't sound too bad until you learn that he was paid a seven-figure advance. That was a storming success compared to footballer Wayne Rooney's book *My Decade in the Premier League*, which sold just 6000 copies in its first six weeks. His advance was £5m.

Whistle-blower Julian Assange, TV presenter and comedian Bill Oddie and actor Christopher Biggins have also experienced disappointing flops in the last few years.

The stars can pull off stunts like these, but the average unknown author, however talented, is likely to spend years trying and failing to find a conventional publisher to take on his books. The reason it's so difficult is that trade publishers are not charities devoted to giving deserving authors a break – they need to make money, and they can only do that by cherry-picking those few books and authors who they believe can sell books by the thousand. They are looking for titles which will shoot off the shelves, with literary merit only a secondary objective (publishers like to build good reputations, but they can't achieve any reputation at all without sales).

A decade or so ago, publishing went through something of a crisis when pressure from the big retail chains forced publishers to cut their lists dramatically; HarperCollins, Time Warner, Penguin, Random House, Pan Macmillan and others all dropped hundreds of decent-selling books from their catalogues, so that they could direct more resources to those titles which could sell in really big numbers and make money despite the ruthlessness of the supermarkets. This focus on mega-bestsellers has not helped moderately successful authors to find deals, even less so new authors.

Naturally trade publishers prefer to take on authors who already have a track record of writing successful books, or who are marketable in their own right, because they are well known, or are acknowledged experts in their field. If course if they do take a risk with an unknown, there's always the chance of hitting the jackpot in return for a very modest initial royalty; there can be no better example than the first Harry Potter book, for which J K Rowling was paid a £2500 advance. A single first-edition copy of that book is now worth ten times that.

But to get back down to earth, here are the main reasons why trade publishers turn down books:

■ They have never heard of you or your work and are not looking for unsolicited new talent.

■ The presentation is clumsy and amateurish and fails to 'sell' you and your book to them.

■ The writing isn't good enough (usually obvious from the first paragraph), either because the writer isn't up to it or hasn't employed an editor, or both.

■ It's blatantly derivative, or what marketing people call a 'me too' product. Consciously or otherwise, the author has used themes and ideas which are already familiar from previously-published bestsellers, films or TV series – an upstairs-downstairs saga, a medieval fantasy about elves and goblins, a swashbuckling spy, a maverick cop on the loose (there is a market for all these kinds of books, but yours had better be good). Remember that *The Lord of the Rings* was (and is) such a success because it was the first of its kind. The same applies to Harry Potter and James Bond.

■ It is too weird, nasty, sick, violent or pornographic.

■ It's not the kind of book people are buying right now, and hence not the kind publishers are looking for, however good it is.

■ You have chosen the wrong publisher for the genre of book you have written.

■ It just isn't sufficiently excellent.

So a book has to look pretty good commercially before a trade publisher will take it on. Consequently the odds against getting your book accepted are very small – a typical publisher might accept a handful of new authors in a year during which they will have sifted through thousands of unsolicited submissions. Sifting means just that; it does not mean reading. There isn't time. A publisher, or a publisher's reader, can tell within a hundred words if a book is going to be any good. If it obviously isn't, those hundred words are all they will ever read.

If you hit the jackpot

If you do secure the holy grail by getting your book accepted by a trade publisher, you will naturally be breaking out the champagne (although given what most authors earn, it's more likely to be a supermarket cava).

So – you made it! Your book has been accepted, and at no cost to you it is going to be published. That's an achievement to be proud of, but please don't give up the day job. First, conventional publishers will expect a fair amount of control over your book, making their own commercial decisions about how it should be edited and designed. They may well want it rewritten, or heavily edited to meet their requirements. They will publish in their own time and often keep authors waiting for many months. And when they have published it, they may pull the plug on it at any time, if it's not selling well. Most trade-published books are out of print within a year or two of publication. Authors whose books have been dropped sometimes approach us to republish them, but there may be little point in reprinting an old book (even if we can get hold of the necessary digital files) unless it is given a fresh look and perhaps a fresh edit, even a new title, and that will probably cost more than it is ever likely to make in sales.

Given that they have put all the money up for producing and marketing your book – which may run into tens of thousands – conventional publishers will expect to keep most of the profits, if there are any. If the book is a best-seller, they will make a lot more gross profit than the author (who will naturally want a better deal for his second book, and will probably get it). If it flops, they'll make a big loss, while the author at least walks away with the advance.

Conventional publishers will want a substantial share of the rights, taking a slice of any further profit opportunities the book offers, in various media and other parts of the world. In today's increasingly cutthroat retail market this share has tended to go up, leaving less and less for the author.

Incidentally, don't assume the rights will revert to you if your book is delisted – they may remain with the publisher, in which case your book will never see the light of day again, unless you can buy them back. An important point to check in looking through your contract. The agreement which thrilled you so much that you wanted to frame it could look, a couple of years later, like nothing more than a set of shackles.

So I need an agent?

Many authors conclude that they should be looking for an agent; he or she will be sure to find a lucrative publishing deal for you while you get on with your next best-seller. Trouble is, just like publishers, agents are extremely choosy – they have to be. They know they will have to spend many hours networking, phoning and emailing to get a deal for even the best book, and like trade publishers, they have to see a return for their investment. So they choose their authors with great care (successful agents pick their authors, not the other way round) and will be working with only a handful of the most commercially promising at any one time. They are unlikely to be interested in new writers unless they have something really exceptional to offer.

Usually agents take their fees from a share of the profits in the book – beware of agents who charge for their services.

Self-publishing

The self-publishing business, generally speaking, is based not on making money from selling books but on producing them for authors. This means the author pays for editing, design and production, but in return you get more control – and potentially more profit.

'For a long time, going the [self-publishing] route repelled critics, publishers – and readers. But as its successes accumulate, so the shame falls away' – The Guardian, *May 14 2015*

Susannah Quinn, who writes sexy women's thrillers, took the self-publishing route and turned down deals when approached by mainstream publishers looking for the next E L James ('Fifty Shades'). She says she has sold 150,000 books in the past year. 'I don't trust publishers to market my books as well as I can, and they take all the rights,' she says. Thriller writer Mark Dawson is earning a six-figure annual pay cheque from Amazon for his novels, while Jasinda Wilder has 'gone trade', signing a seven-figure deal with Berkley Books (part of Penguin Random House, the world's biggest publisher) after selling more than two million eBooks under her own steam.

However to most authors, self-publishing is simply the only way of publishing a book which is not of interest to the trade. In contrast to conventional publishing, where getting a book accepted can seem all but impossible, the self-publishing bar is low, even absent. Self-publishers tend to accept most submissions, once the manuscript has been brought to a publishable standard.

A good self-publisher should be able to turn your MS into a book which is good enough to stand alongside the best-sellers on the retailers' shelves. Naturally, doing it properly does not come cheap – you'll be looking at an outlay comfortably into four figures, because of the amount of professional time involved. They will also share the editing and design process with the author, taking into account his/her preferences. They will work to your deadlines, not the other way round, and they should give you the bulk of profits from sales – the publisher's money comes primarily from the editing and production fees you pay. They will normally also allow you to keep the rights. So if you manage to self-publish a best-seller, you will make a lot more money than you could with a trade publisher. It's a big if, of course.

We are often asked to republish a book that's already out there, or publish one that has been dropped by a trade publisher, in the hope that this will bring it the sales it has been missing. If it is properly repackaged, with perhaps a new title, and then promoted correctly, that's quite possible. However the cost of re-editing, redesigning and marketing is not likely to be covered by new sales unless the book is very commercial (and if it has been delisted by a trade publisher, it probably isn't).

Crossover publishing

The division between trade publishing and self-publishing is becoming less clear-cut. US-based book data specialist Bowker reported in September 2016: "More authors are opting for a hybrid approach to book publishing. Rather than committing exclusively to self-publication or going through a traditional publishing house, authors choose the best method for their work, depending on type of book, sales market, or target audience."

Reflecting this development towards 'crossover' publishing (my phrase), one of the key changes in self-publishing is that today some of most forward-thinking houses, including the one I work for, may agree to contribute to the initial cost of producing a book or even agree to produce it at their own expense, IF they believe it has a real chance of making a profit for themselves as well as the author. This is great for the talented author who does not have the funds to pay for a standard self-publishing deal but whose book (or books) is good enough to make a small splash and perhaps notch up a few thousand sales.

Self-publishing a full-length book properly, including editing (but not, of course, promoting it), typically costs a couple of thousand pounds or more* depending on how long it is, how much work the text needs and how much illustration is involved. You may have discovered that there are companies around who will publish your book for you for substantially less than this. What's the catch?

No one can edit, design and publish a full-length book properly on a three-figure budget. Producing a book to professional standards involves professional time – and plenty of it. A bargain price can only mean that very little professional time will be spent on your book, because the time of professionals in editing and designing your book has to be paid for.

Will an experienced editor be carrying out a proper check and edit of the text, then giving you a chance to approve it and make revisions? Few manuscripts are good enough to publish without editing, but editing is a time-consuming (and hence costly) process and some self-publishers try to avoid doing it properly – or at all, as mentioned above.

And will your book be individually designed by a specialist book designer, with an entirely original cover, to a standard that's good enough for sale in the bookshops? The cheaper publishers tend to dig into a limited library of scenic views and slap the first thing that looks like a reasonable fit onto the cover. The result is a dull and amateurish cover which has no real relevance to the book. A specialist book designer should be able to come up with a cover design which picks up on key points in the story and looks as good as anything the trade can do.

Some companies are able to offer genuinely low prices by focusing their service on very short books, as short as 5-10,000 words. As far as the market's concerned that isn't really a book at all, but it may be OK if you have a very short memoir and just want copies for friends and family.

Chances are a self-publisher who quotes very low prices is using one of the automated platforms which exist for this purpose, which brings me to…

DIY publishing

By far the cheapest way of producing a book is to do it yourself using automated software, from editing to design, buying in only the print. There are two major platforms which allow you to do this – Amazon's CreateSpace, and Lulu. Both systems allow authors to manage the publishing process themselves at very low cost, all the way to printing or creating eBook files, and low-budget publishers often use it on their clients' behalf.

Lulu and CreateSpace are simple, accessible platforms which bring publishing a book within the reach of anyone who has some ability with a computer and a few hundred pounds to spend. Anyone can use them to produce a book cheaply and quickly, but the final product will be only as well edited and designed as the skills of the author allow. The trade accepts only books published to professional standards; trying to get them to accept a Lulu-produced book would be a bit like trying to sell your home-made fudge to Marks & Spencer. Also, the trade, ie the various outlets which stock, distribute and sell books, takes its information electronically from publishers using very sophisticated data feeds. CreateSpace is geared only to publishing on Amazon, while Lulu gives only limited access to the trade.

Check for bricks and mortar

Some of the largest self-publishing firms advertising in the UK are US-based (though this is not clear from their websites) and may not offer the same individual and personal service to a UK author as a good British-based publishing house. When you're looking at a self-publisher's website, try to see if there is a UK street address in evidence. If not, the chances are they're an international company based in the States.

You should make sure your prospective publisher can provide all the services you need – production of eBook files, uploading to all the main retail websites, ISBN registration etc. Some companies don't, particularly those whose core business is printing rather than publishing.

The hidden charges

Some self-publishing companies are not particularly open about the way they charge. They may pretend to 'accept' a manuscript as if they're going to publish it at their own expense, but after 'reviewing' it they will ask for payment. The author may imagine the publisher is going to make their money from sales of the book. The publisher knows this is unlikely. Trouble is, the author feels locked in and doesn't like to back out, so he reaches for his chequebook. After all, he thinks, they are going to publish my book – I mustn't upset them.

More questions to ask

Does the company have an arrangement with a UK distributor and a sales team who can place their books in the trade, giving them a chance to sell appropriate books through the shops? Very few self-publishing houses can offer this.

What do their authors say about them? A good publisher will be able to show plenty of positive testimonials. To check the company out, try googling its name plus 'review' to find out what their customers say. And finally, how good are their books? Look up some of their titles and see if they have been reviewed, and if so, if the reviews are any good.

It's not surprising that an increasing number of established authors are now taking the self-publishing route alongside those who simply want a book out for personal reasons. They know they will have far more say over the way their book is edited, designed and published, and if it's successful it can make far more money, because the author should get most of the profits.

This does of course mean that the author's work is not finished when the book is published – if you want sales, you're going to have to promote and publicise it. More about that in Chapter 19.

CHAPTER 18

Working with a publisher

When you're submitting material to a conventional publisher, one who is going to pay for editing, designing and producing your book, most of the decisions are down to them. They will consult you on, for example, making changes to the text, but they're likely to take the view that as they're paying, they're going to call the shots. They might tell you to make the book shorter or longer, or ditch characters, or rewrite passages. The same applies to the design of the book; they will feel they know best (as indeed, they do).

When you send your manuscript to a self-publishing house, on the other hand, you're the client, so you have a lot more say. That doesn't mean that going the self-publishing route allows you to publish any old book just because you're paying. A good self-publisher, one with a reputation to maintain, will not agree to put out a book which will disappoint readers – one which doesn't make sense, or has not been properly edited, or has an amateurish cover design.

To enable your self-publisher to do a good job for you, start by telling them something about the background to the book and what your plans are for it. Is it is just for the family, or do you hope to sell it commercially? Has it already been edited by a third party? Is it all your own work? Has it been published before by another firm?

Don't expect an editor to actually *read* your book before initially responding – if publishers read every manuscript sent to them, they would never get home to their families, let alone do any work. To have a professional read your book and report on it, you will have to pay a fee. A self-publishing editor will start by giving you a free outline assessment, skimming through it and sampling passages to see how much editing is needed, and what kind. Then he will be able to advise you of the likely costs. Subtle issues such as problems with the plot and characters (if it's fiction) won't emerge without a proper read-through, for which you'll have to pay. The editor should then discuss with you what's to be done, who will do it and what it will cost.

The editor's job

So you need to be clear what you want from your chosen publisher. Are you happy with your book, and just feel it needs tidying up? Or are you inviting an editor to tear it apart and rebuild it, or to help you to do so? He might not give you a choice, if he feels the story doesn't work and is not prepared to publish it as it stands. But provided the basic ideas and material are there (and you have the budget), a good editor can do almost anything with a manuscript, fixing problems with the plot, making characters more credible and transforming muddled, plodding, ungrammatical prose into a sharp narrative that will make the book a page-turner.

Fees will be based not just on the editing time but the time likely to be taken up with your further revisions and amendments, your various enquiries, discussions with the studio and dealing with design, cover text etc. A good self-publishing house will be willing to attend to all these things, rather than simply whizzing your book through a brief assessment and a spellcheck.

In working on a factual book, the editor should point out to the author any passages where something has not been fully explained and more detail or more colour is called for; you should also be told where your manuscript is too wordy or goes into irrelevant detail. A good editor will also pick up and correct errors of fact, such as misspelled place names or erroneous historical references.

More subtly, the editor will alert you to creative problems which really need to be addressed by you as author. Editors can't develop characters, tweak the plot or add creative description – or at least, if they do they are not editing so much as rewriting, bringing in their own ideas and creativity, so it's no longer entirely the author's book. But the editor will tell the author if these elements are not working properly, for example if characters are not differentiated – eg (very common in romantic novels) the principal female characters are all beautiful and haughty and the men are handsome and devious. And a big hole in the plot which the author may not have noticed should be immediately obvious to an editor, mainly because he/she is seeing your prose as a reader would, with fresh and critical eyes.

The various kinds of editing process may be handled serially or all at the same time, depending partly on the available budget. A **structural edit** is a fundamental review of the manuscript, covering every aspect of it, from vocabulary to characterisation. The editor will look for errors, inconsistencies, issues which are not explained properly, stylistic problems, a confused plot, poor description or limited use of language. He/she will suggest adding material where for example a setting has not been described clearly, or deleting passages where the story goes off at a tangent. A structural edit is a big job – on a full-length book it is likely to take several days at least, and cost accordingly.

Copy editing focuses on the detail, correcting grammatical and syntactical errors, narrative order and exposition (the way the story is told). Errors such as spelling mistakes and wrongly-constructed sentences will usually be corrected at this stage, but in case they are not...

Proofreading is an additional process to follow editing, used routinely by trade publishers but less frequently by self-publishing firms because of the cost, which in the case of self-publishing has to be borne by the author. Many new authors tend to confuse it with editing, but it is quite different; a proofreader's job is to pick up errors in spelling, grammar, typesetting, punctuation, capitalisation, spacing, paragraphing, indexing, formatting of headings, captioning etc, and to ensure the manuscript has been faithfully reproduced with nothing missing, whereas an editor's aim is to improve the MS much more fundamentally by dealing with such problems as a confused narrative, unnatural direct speech, clumsy style or sentence construction, repetition, poor choice of vocabulary and problems with content, exposition or description. Of course editors do also correct spelling mistakes, punctuation etc, but proofreading puts a final magnifying glass over the text before it is committed to the presses. It is expensive however, so a good alternative, if you know someone who has a precise knowledge of English and a keen eye for mistakes, is to ask them to do the job for you (as mentioned in chapter 16). But please make sure they don't try to edit the book all over again – you are just looking for hard errors that may have been missed.

When your edited text comes back for you to check, the chances are you will have a few changes and comments to make before you're happy to sign it off. But do respect the editor's expertise. If you think he/she has introduced an error in spelling, punctuation, grammar, capitalisation etc, check before correcting it back. Otherwise your time and the editor's may be wasted. Older authors in particular are sometimes very set in their ways and reluctant to accept that their lifelong writing habits may not actually be correct. We have frequently had capital letters put back where we had corrected them to lower case, hyphens put back into compound nouns that don't use them and correctly-placed commas rearranged wrongly by authors who felt they knew best. One manuscript I worked on had full stops in front of every closing quotation mark, even when it wasn't the end of the sentence. I took them all out – there were several hundred – before sending it to the author for sign-off. When I got the MS back I found they had all been put back in again.

Remember that if you're self-publishing and you make changes (as opposed to minor corrections) after the editor has started work, you run the risk of incurring extra charges; if you make corrections after a typographer has started work, they are a near certainty.

Unfortunately, no book is ever entirely finished. However careful you are, one or two minor errors are sure to pop out at you or your readers after the book has been published. Some authors insist on re-reading and tweaking until they have driven their poor publisher to distraction. Sooner or later you are going to have to remind yourself that there is no such thing as perfection in publishing, and force yourself to leave the damn thing alone.

Showing changes

Word has a very good system for showing alterations called Track Changes. In the later versions you can hide your changes as you work, and then reveal them any time you want to see them. This enables us to let the author see what we have done to their manuscript. However, making changes to an MS which has already been altered in Track Changes by someone else can be confusing, so we also send a plain version of the text, inviting the author to refer to the Track Changes file only to check what the editor has done. When authors make changes to an edited document, we find it easier if rather than use Track Changes they simply alter the plain text file as they wish, then colour the altered lines red so we can spot them and check them. If you make substantial changes to an edited text without showing them, the editor may have to check the whole MS again, and you'll be charged for the extra work.

The design of your book

If you have an artistic bent, you may be planning to design your own cover – there's plenty of software out there that will let you. Unfortunately it's harder than you think to create a good cover, particularly one which will make the public take your book seriously. The standard is set by the books you see on the bookshop shelves, and it's high. For the book to have any chance of selling to the world at large, your cover needs to be that good. It isn't just a question of impact and aesthetic appeal; it has to work both close up and at thumbnail size. It must give the book a strong identity, and like the title, it should reflect the tone and subject matter.

The publisher may be happy to take your ideas on board and incorporate an image supplied by you if appropriate, but book design is a highly specialised job for which many technical and visual parameters must be taken into account, and it really needs to be left to the professionals, using professional book-design software – not Microsoft Publisher or Photoshop, for example.

Wander into a bookshop and pick up a paperback. That photo on the cover of an angry blonde holding a knife wasn't shot for the book – it was purchased and downloaded from a professional image library. It will have been manipulated to match the brief for the cover, with eg a black dress instead of the original green. The knife will be a separate image, also purchased from a library, and so are the windows glinting in the background. This is because most covers are designed by 'comping' together selected existing images to capture the atmosphere and theme of the book. If the designer wants to show, for example, a young soldier in a desert battle, he'll find a suitable background image of a desert landscape in roughly the right part of the world, plus maybe a tank or an exploding bomb, and a picture of a soldier who broadly matches the subject (whether fact or fiction) for age, race etc. If you start telling us you like the man but his hair should be slightly longer or he's wearing the wrong boots, it's going to get tricky, because the designer will have to discard that image and look again, for a picture that probably doesn't exist. If the picture has to be very specific the only answer may be original illustration or studio photography, which will add massively to the cost.

Authors with artistic ability may well be able to make a valuable contribution to the way their cover looks, as long as they are not too prescriptive. Telling the designer your cover has to have a purple mongoose at the top of the page and two oak trees at the bottom with the text in orange won't get you a very good result. Telling him you want the cover to suggest loneliness, jungle heat or urban decay is much more likely to set him on the path to a design that will do a good job.

If you do submit a home-grown cover design and the publisher accepts it without challenge, you should be suspicious – they may simply be taking the easy option and saving themselves the trouble and expense of doing the job properly. Remember, self-publishers do not rely on selling your book to make money, because they know that most of their books will have very modest sales.

Along with the cover, the designer will prepare artwork for the text of the book, using a suitable font, setting and type area. If you have particular requirements here, such as keeping it legible for older eyes, you should tell the publisher, but again, you need to trust the professionals – they know what they are doing, or should do. If the book is long, setting it in a larger font may result in a book the size of a telephone directory. It may be worth asking them to typeset just a few pages first and show them to you, in case you don't like the treatment.

The publishing process

Once you have approved the text and the design, the book will be signed off for printing. There is bound to be a certain delay before a) you receive your copies b) it is listed on Amazon and the other retail sites and c) anyone actually buys it. It is likely to be several months before you receive information about sales and eventually, royalties. Publishing is a protracted business, though with a good self-publishing house it is a good deal less protracted than it used to be. The whole cycle, typically, from submission of text for editing to availability on the market, could be completed in a couple of months, but if there are delays along the way because of a need for revisions or new material, for example, it may take considerably longer. The publisher will have allocated certain time slots for work on your book and if you send it back requiring extra work which was never planned, there may be a delay – you can't expect them to drop everything at short notice to spend an unplanned few hours on your book.

As mentioned, one of the key differences between self-publishing and conventional publishing is that self-publishers do not have the same vested interest in selling your book, because they make their money from fees for editing, design and production. A trade publisher has to market your book to get a return – a self-publisher doesn't. But a good self-publisher will want its books to do as well as possible and accordingly should be prepared to help its authors to promote their books, by for example printing publicity flyers and helping them with internet marketing techniques. The good news, of course, is that with self-publishing the author will get a far better return for every copy sold.

CHAPTER 19

Getting your book noticed

Getting your book published and 'out there' is just the start. If sales are important to you, you still have a lot of work to do. A good publisher will help and advise you, but remember that self-publishers, generally speaking, do not make their money from sales, so unless you have agreed with them that they will market your book for you in return for a share of the proceeds, you are the one who needs to make sales happen. Giving your self-publisher a hard time because your book isn't selling is a bit like complaining to a picture framer when no one buys your paintings.

There are essentially three ways your book might get sold – through the internet, through bookshops and directly by the author.

Selling through the internet

On-line sales are vital for most self-published authors, as their books are less likely to be accepted by the trade and stocked in bookshops. Amazon is now overwhelmingly in charge of the book market, so for most people, publishing a book means a listing there.

Whoever publishes your book, they will probably put it on Amazon more or less automatically. The publisher will upload digital files for the book to Amazon, who will use them to print copies on demand to meet orders. Only if your book is selling in quantity will Amazon want copies to be supplied in bulk by the publisher.

Amazon lists a sales ranking for each book (look under 'Product Details' at the bottom). Given that it lists several million titles, you might think a ranking of say 50,000 is not bad, and suggests your book is selling in reasonable numbers. In fact (although Amazon don't elaborate on how their rankings equate to sales) it would appear that only the top 10,000 or so titles sell in any quantity. Books rated lower than that will be selling only a handful of a copies a week at best. The sale of just a couple of books can suddenly shoot your ranking up by several hundred thousand places, but if it's still in five or six figures, it ain't time to give up the day job yet.

Selling through the trade

The bookstores do not, on the whole, buy self-published books. They are interested only in the most commercial titles, usually handled by conventional (trade) publishers and supplied to the shops through a very small number of wholesalers who control the book trade. This means there are only two ways you will ever sell a book through, for example, Waterstones – by getting it accepted by a trade distributor supplying these wholesalers, or by coming to an arrangement personally with a particular store which has a reason to stock your book, usually because it is about that particular area or you are well known in the town. Mereo is unusual among self-publishing companies in having an arrangement with a distributor who will place suitable books with the trade. Most self-publishing companies do not have this direct entrée to the trade, and their only sales come through Amazon etc, or via the author.

Naturally distributors will take only the most commercially-promising books, those they expect to sell in reasonable numbers, and if they don't want your book, that is their decision. No one can force your book into the trade.

There is at least a six-month lead time for trade distribution, because they plan well in advance, so you need to see the publishing of a commercial book as a fairly long-drawn out process.

Please note that the retailers expect to buy books in for no more than 40-45% of the cover price. So on a book retailing at say £12, they might pay the author or publisher £5. There won't be much left from that by the time you have paid for printing and delivery. Authors often suggest that their books should be sold for say £7.99 to encourage sales. It may well do that, but the £3.50 or so the retailer would pay for copies might not even cover the printing cost. In the trade, such prices are only possible with big-selling titles which are printed by the thousand, often overseas. Most of the books you see on sale in the shops have been printed like this.

How many copies will your book sell?

This of course is the $64,000 question (if only such sums had anything to do with most publishing returns). We hear on the news of books selling hundreds of thousands, even millions of copies, and the author tends to imagine that if *Fifty Shades of Grey* could sell 100 million copies then surely his/her own rather similar offering, *Twenty Tones of Pink*, should at least sell 1 per cent of that.

The truth is that even a hundredth of one per cent of *Fifty Shades'* sales would be a spectacular result for a work of fiction by an unknown author. With a couple of hundred thousand books being published in the UK alone each year and several million titles on Amazon, there just isn't room for most books to sell more than a few hundred copies at best. Authors often assume that all their friends will buy a copy. They may tell the author they will (they often pretend they already have), but when the sales figures come back, the bitter truth emerges. The actual sales figure could be lower than the number of people claiming to have bought the book. The computer and the services of self-publishing companies have put publishing a book within the range of most of us, but they have not increased the number of people who are out there to buy them.

Having said all that, if your book is indeed original, topical, funny, sexy, shocking, enlightening, moving or inspiring – the sort of book that gets talked about – it could sell thousands of copies, particularly if people start recommending it to their friends and posting enthusiastic reviews on line, or if you are very well known. But that's unusual. And however good it is, your book is unlikely to sell in any quantity without investment in promotion, and possibly not even then.

How to help your book to sell

Fortunately there are lots of things an author can do to get people to notice their book and start notching up some sales. Here are some of them.

Direct marketing

You'll have heard this term before. It means targeting the consumer directly one to one – unsolicited marketing, eg emails, letters and leaflet drops. It needs to be carefully targeted, to the sort of people who would find your book appealing.

Public relations

If you can sell yourself to the buying public, sales of your book are likely to follow. This works best if you are well-known in a particular field – climbing, say, or horticulture or archaeology – and can make personal appearances to the kind of groups who share an interest in your subject.

Using a specialist **PR consultancy** will involve some financial outlay, but it can make an enormous difference by targeting stories about your book to the right media, and the right journalists. A few column inches in the right places can suddenly create a demand for you and your book. But it will only work well if the book – and you – are interesting enough for them. There are more opportunities to promote factual books, particularly topical ones, than fiction.

If you're doing your PR yourself, phone your local **radio station** and tell them about your book and ask if they would like to interview you on air. If you are having a book promotion you could also take the opportunity to advertise it on local commercial radio. Organise the event well in advance and check that the radio station is willing to record an interview with you beforehand.

Phone your local paper's **newsdesk** and tell them you are a local author and that your book has just been published (of course you should wait until copies are available, even if the book hasn't actually been released yet). Before you call, jot down a list of the points you want to be sure to mention – the title of the book, when it's coming out, your name as it appears on the book and the URL of a website where it can be purchased.

Check out your local **library** and see what local magazines are available that might be interested in your book; the librarian might have a list for you to copy.

Try the **specialist press**. A book about aircraft probably won't get coverage in the national news media, but it might get space in a magazine devoted to aircraft, and the same applies to any subject which has associated titles dedicated to it – sport, natural history, cookery, warfare etc.

Try to get people to **review** your book, and then use your best reviews in publicity. Getting into the literary pages of the national newspapers will prove a tall order for the average new writer, but most local papers and specialist magazines review appropriate titles from time to time, so if yours is up their street, send it to them. There are of course many websites that review books.

On Amazon, reader reviews help enormously in selling a book, and books with none are unlikely to attract sales. Note that Amazon does not allow authors or their 'family members or close friends' to post reviews of their own products, and will remove them if it suspects foul play.

Unfortunately, irresponsible reviewing on Amazon isn't confined to phoney praise; it's not unusual for an author to be the victim of an unfairly negative or ill-informed review. I don't know why people do this – maybe to undermine the competition, or out of spite or jealousy, or simply because they like throwing their weight around (anonymously of course) – but I wish Amazon would do more to deter the serial bad-mouthers. A reader who reviewed one book we published, by the father of a young police officer murdered on the job, thought the book should have dealt with all the other officers who have died on duty, while another was tactless enough to criticise the author for complaining that his wife was not at first allowed to see her stepdaughter's body. Fortunately a number of more sensible readers posted reviews pointing out what ridiculous and insensitive complaints these were.

Another review of a book I worked on (by a professional writer) accused it of being full of spelling mistakes and grammatical errors. In fact the review contained more errors than the book. Fortunately many of the Amazon trolls are barely literate, which should help to tell readers how seriously such comments should be taken.

Amazon won't remove a review unless there is something dishonest about it – they won't delete it just because it is unfairly critical. If you do get hit by a nasty, unfair review, don't let it get to you. You could invite your followers to respond by posting positive reviews of their own, if they haven't done so already – a few good reviews will make a lone whinger look isolated. Then forget about it and concentrate on your next book.

"I learned long ago never to wrestle with a pig. You get dirty, and besides, the pig likes it." – George Bernard Shaw

Bookstores

The bookshops are very choosy about what they put on their shelves, as they can only stock a tiny fraction of the millions of books on the market. However local bookstores are often willing to stock a small supply of books by local authors, especially if you explain that you're telling local people to get their copy there. They may be prepared to let you put on a book signing event. If so, they may want you to bring your own books and charge you a fee, or they may prefer to buy a number of the books and keep the profit from them.

As mentioned, it's difficult for the self-published author to make money from sales to bookshops, so they are best regarded as part of your publicity campaign rather than a route to royalties.

Online opportunities

The internet provides a host of opportunities to plug your book, and your audience is unlimited. Get yourself a website, or create a Facebook page, or both. You might also try establishing a following on Twitter, or starting a blog (weblog).

There is pretty much nothing you can't put on YouTube, including your book. Get a friend with the necessary skills to film you talking about it, in an apt setting. If you're good at putting yourself across in an entertaining way, this could work very well, because an interesting author will imply the book is interesting too. But it works the other way too, so don't try this if you think you're going to come across as boring or nervous.

A hotel launch

Check out your local hotels and see what they'll charge for the use of a small conference rooms for a few hours. Consider the kind of person your book is aimed at and work out whether they would be able to come in the morning, afternoon or evening – do they work, are they retired, will they be away on holiday? July and August is not the best time.

Ask the hotel what they will supply in the way of food. Can your guests use the bar? Will they provide waiting staff etc? This all depends on how big you want to go, what your budget is and your intended customers. If you have a few close friends who are happy to help, this will be a bonus. Many people who launch books this way invite as many friends and family as possible and tell them to bring their friends too, to make it look busy and successful.

Promote the event by phoning, emailing and writing to your friends and contacts asking if they will support you. Announce it in the local paper, on the local radio or through flyers and posters. Put posters up in appropriate places – for example if it's a romantic novel for women you might target local hairdressing salons or fashion shops, or if it's about football, the local sports shops.

Local organisations

Your book may have special interest for some local club or organisation, depending on the subject – a local history society, sports club or church body. Or they may be interested in you because of who you are, the job you do or some public post you hold. Depending on your book's subject, you may well find societies happy to take you for a speaking engagement – eg churches, reading circles, book clubs, Women's Institutes, arts groups and history societies. Your local library may like you to arrange a reading session, especially if it is a children's book. Target your market. You may find that societies in other areas would be happy to give you a speaking engagement. If it's a book about some aspect of business, you could offer to speak at a conference on the subject.

Is your book about the area where you live or where you were brought up? Then maybe the relevant Tourist Information Centre or National Trust shop would take a few copies on sale or return (bear in mind that like the bookstores, they will pay you only a fraction of the retail price.)

Check out conferences and meetings relevant to your subject. They often have book displays – for example big Christian get-togethers tend to have bookstalls during and after the event, so if your book deals with God and Christianity you could take a stand.

REFERENCES

Where to find out more

BOOKS

The Writers' and Artists' Yearbook (published annually by A&C Black)

The Writers' and Artists' Yearbook Guide to How To Write, Harry Bingham (Bloomsbury)

The Writers' and Artists' Yearbook Guide to Getting Published, Harry Bingham (Bloomsbury)

How Not to Write a Novel, Sandra Newman and Howard Mittelmark (Penguin)

The Art of Fiction, David Lodge (Penguin)

From Pitch to Publication, Carole Blake (Macmillan)

Writing a Novel and Getting Published, Nigel Watts (Teach Yourself Books, Hodder & Stoughton)

Bestseller, Celia Brayfield (Fourth Estate)

How to Get Published and Make a Lot of Money, Susan Page (Piatkus, USA)

The Ultimate Guide to Writing and Marketing a Bestselling Book on a Shoestring Budget, Dee Blick (Filament)

Wannabe a Writer? Jane Wenham-Jones (Accent Press)

The Art of Writing Fiction, Andrew Cowan (Longman)

The Business of Writing for Children, Aaron Shepard (Shepard Publications)

How to Write for Children and Get Published, Louise Jordan
(Piatkus Books)

*Eats, Shoots and Leaves, the zero tolerance approach to
punctuation*, Lynne Truss (Profile Books)

The Penguin Dictionary of English Grammar, R L Trask
(Penguin)

Bill Bryson's Dictionary for Writers and Editors, Bill Bryson
(Black Swan)

USEFUL WEBSITES

Society of Authors:
www.societyofauthors.org

The Society for Editors and Proofreaders:
http://www.sfep.org.uk/

The British Library:
www.bl.uk (www.writersandartists.co.uk

www.firstwriter.com (a useful site for new writers)

www.wordribbon.tips.net
(Microsoft's guide to using Word for writers)

Writers' and Artists' Yearbook:
www.writersandartists.co.uk

The Publishers' Association (market information):
www.publishers.org.uk

www.sellingbooks.com

Book design:
www.wikipedia.org/wiki/Book_design

Copyright (UK):
https://www.copyrightservice.co.uk/copyright/p01_uk_copyrig
ht_law

Punctuation:
http://www.sussex.ac.uk/informatics/punctuation/

http://www.oxforddictionaries.com/words/punctuation-in-
direct-speech

Contact the author at:
chris@chrisnewton.co.uk
www.chrisnewton.co.uk

APPENDIX I

The principal publishing genres

The book trade allocates every title to one of a fixed list of genres (awkward word, but it's the one the trade uses), so to be accepted and marketed correctly your book needs to fit one of them. Many books may have relevance to more than one genre, for example a war book with a historical theme, but it will be listed under just one heading, so you have to know which you are targeting. The genres each have sub-genres, sometimes dozens of them (for example computers/computer animation, computers / computer architecture, computers / computer engineering etc), and the full list has around 3000 entries. These are the main trade genre categories.

Fiction

General
Action & Adventure
Biographical
Christian/General
Coming of Age
Contemporary Women
Crime
Cultural Heritage
Dystopian
Erotica
Fairy Tales, Folk Tales, Legends & Mythology
Family Life
Gay
Ghost
Gothic
Graphic Novels
Historical
Horror
Humorous
Lesbian
Literary
Mystery & Detective
Noir
Religious
Romance
Romance/Historical
Sagas
Satire
Science Fiction

Sea Stories
Short Stories (Multiple Authors)
Short Stories (Single Author)
Sports
Superheroes
Television Tie-In
Thrillers/General
War & Military
Westerns

Non-fiction

Antiques & Collectibles
Architecture
Biography & Autobiography
Body, Mind & Spirit
Business & Economics
Computers
Cooking
Crafts & Hobbies
Drama
Education
Family & Relationships
Foreign Language Study
Games
Gardening
Health & Fitness
History
House & Home
Humour
Juvenile Fiction

Juvenile Non-fiction

Language, Arts & Disciplines

Law

Literary Collections

Literary Criticism

Mathematics

Medical

Music

Nature

Performing Arts

Pets

Philosophy

Photography

Poetry

Political Science

Psychology

Reference

Religion

Science

Self-Help

Social Science

Sports & Recreation

Study Aids

Technology

Transportation

Travel

True Crime

Non-Classifiable

Best-selling books

The 20 best-selling books so far of 2016 (as of November 2016) according to UK Business Insider (uk.businessinsider.com)

1   *Harry Potter and the Cursed Child*, J K Rowling (junior fiction)

2   *Strengths Finder 2.0*, by Tom Rath (self-help)

3   *Oh, the Places You'll Go*, by Dr Seuss (children)

4   *The Life-Changing Magic of Tidying Up: the Japanese Art of Decluttering and Organizing*, by Marie Kondo (self-help)

5   *First 100 Words*, by Roger Priddy (young children)

6   *When Breath Becomes Air*, by Paul Kalanithi (memoir)

7   *The 5 Love Languages: The Secret to Love that Lasts*, by Gary Chapman (self-help)

8   *The Whole 30: The 30-Day Guide to Total Health and Food Freedom*, by Melissa and Dallas Hartwig (self-help)

9   *How to Win Friends & Influence People, by Dale Carnegie* (self-help)

10   *To Kill a Mockingbird*, by Harper Lee (fiction)

11= *Mindset: The New Psychology of Success*, by Carol Dweck (self-help)

11= *Official SAT Study Guide (2016 Edition),* by The College Board (self-help/education)

13   *The Constitution of the United States* (politics/affairs)

14   *Hamilton: The Revolution*, by Lin-Manuel Miranda and Jeremy McCarter (the book of a Broadway show)

15   *The 7 Habits of Highly Effective People: Powerful Lessons in Personal Change*, by Stephen R. Covey (self-help)

16= *The Four Agreements: A Practical Guide to Personal Freedom*, by Don Miguel Ruiz (self-help)

16= *The Very Hungry Caterpillar*, by Eric Carle (young children)

18   *Stress Relief Coloring Book: Garden Designs, Mandalas, Animals, and Paisley Patterns* (art/self-help)

19   *Between the World and Me*, by Ta-Nehisi Coates (memoir, social commentary)

20   *Adult Coloring Books: A Coloring Book for Adults Featuring Mandalas and Henna Inspired Flowers, Geometry, and Paisley Patterns* (art/self-help)

Books published in English which have sold 50 million copies or more

1 *Don Quixote*, Miguel de Cervantes (500 million)

2 *A Tale of Two Cities*, Charles Dickens (200 million)

3 *The Lord of the Rings*, JRR Tolkien (150 million)

4 *The Hobbit*, JRR Tolkien (140 million)

5 *The Little Prince*, Antoine de Saint-Exupéry (140 million)

6 *Harry Potter and the Philosopher's Stone*, JK Rowling (107 million)

7 *And Then There Were None,* Agatha Christie (100 million)

8 *Alice in Wonderland*, Lewis Carroll (100 million)

9 *The Lion, the Witch and the Wardrobe*, CS Lewis (85 million)

10 *She: A History of Adventure*, H Rider Haggard (83 million)

11 *The Da Vinci Code*, Dan Brown (80 million)

12 *Think and Grow Rich*, Napoleon Hill (70 million)

13 *Harry Potter and the Half-Blood Prince*, JK Rowling (65 million)

14 *The Catcher in the Rye*, JD Salinger (65 million)

15 *The Adventures of Sherlock Holmes*, Sir Arthur Conan Doyle (60 million)

16 *20,000 Leagues Under the Sea*, Jules Verne (60 million)

17 *Harry Potter and the Chamber of Secrets*, JK Rowling (60 million)

18 *Harry Potter and the Prisoner of Azkaban*, JK Rowling (55 million)

19 *Harry Potter and the Goblet of Fire*, JK Rowling (55 million)

20 *Harry Potter and the Order of the Phoenix*, JK Rowling (55 million)

21 *Harry Potter and the Deathly Hallows*, JK Rowling (50 million)

22 *Lolita,* Vladimir Nabokov (50 million)

23 *The Common Sense Book of Baby and Child Care*, Dr Benjamin Spock (50 million)

24 *Anne of Green Gables*, Lucy Maud Montgomery (50 million)

25 *Black Beauty*, Anna Sewell (50 million)

26 *Men Are From Mars, Women Are From Venus*, John Gray (50 million)

27 *The Eagle Has Landed*, Jack Higgins (50 million)

28 *Watership Down*, Richard Adams (50 million)

29 *The Hite Report*, Shere Hite (50 million)

30 *Charlotte's Web*, EB White (50 million)

31 *The Ginger Man*, JP Donleavy (50 million)

32 *The Bridges of Madison County*, Robert James Waller (50 million)

33 *Ben Hur*, Lew Wallace (50 million)

34 *The Mark of Zorro*, Johnston McCulley (50 million)

APPENDIX III

Transatlantic spellings

Many American spellings have unconsciously become accepted in the UK, so there is a grey (or gray) area between words which are always spelled (spelt) the British way in the UK and those for which either spelling is accepted. Below are most of the words which are still subject to a clear US-UK divide.

AMERICAN	ENGLISH
Aluminum	Aluminium
Analyze	Analyse
Annex	Annexe
Barbeque	Barbecue
Behavior	Behaviour
Blond	Blonde
Burglarised	Burgled

AMERICAN	ENGLISH
Center	Centre
Check	Cheque
Chiseled	Chiselled
Curb (of road)	Kerb
Defense	Defence
Dialed	Dialled
Disk	Disc
Draft	Draught (of air)
Endeavor	Endeavour
Favorite	Favourite
Fiber	Fibre
Flavor	Flavour
Fetus	Foetus
Fulfil	Fulfill
Gray	Grey
Grueling	Gruelling
Harbor	Harbour
Honor	Honour
Humor	Humour
Jewelry	Jewellery
Labeled	Labelled
Labor	Labour
License (noun)	Licence
Maneuver	Manoeuvre
Marveled	Marvelled
Marvelous	Marvellous
Meager	Meagre
Meter	Metre
Mold	Mould
Mollusk	Mollusc
Mustache	Moustache

AMERICAN	ENGLISH
Neighbor	Neighbour
Odor	Odour
Omelet	Omelette
Pajamas	Pyjamas
Parlor	Parlour
Plow	Plough
Practice (verb)	Practise
Pretense	Pretence
Program	Programme
Rigor	Rigour
Rumor	Rumour
Sanitarium	Sanatorium
Savor	Savour
Skeptic	Sceptic
Smolder	Smoulder
Somber	Sombre
Sometime	Some time
Story	Storey (of building)
Sulfur	Sulphur*
Swiveled	Swivelled
Tire	Tyre
Tranquility	Tranquillity
Traveled/Traveling	Travelled/Travelling
Tumor	Tumour
Woolen	Woollen

*But note that the scientific community has recently adopted 'sulfur' rather than 'sulphur' as the international spelling.